ESSENTIALS

EVERYDAY ETIQUETTE

PEGGY POST

HarperPaperbacks
A Division of HarperCollins*Publishers*

HarperPaperbacks
A Division of HarperCollins*Publishers*
10 East 53rd Street, New York, NY 10022-5299

ISBN 0-06-273663-9

HarperCollins®, ■®, and HarperPaperbacks™ are trademarks of HarperCollins Publishers Inc.

First Harper Paperbacks printing: July 1999

Printed in the United States of America

Visit HarperPaperbacks on the World Wide Web at
http://www.harpercollins.com

❖ 10 9 8 7 6 5 4 3 2 1

CONTENTS

INTRODUCTION

Modern life can get awfully complicated. I am aware of this confusion firsthand, since I'm asked so many questions by people who want to know how to interact courteously with others in an ever-changing and rushed world. Questions like: "Is it okay to use e-mail as a party invitation?" Or: "Is it still necessary for a man to open doors for ladies?" Many people are hungry for answers to family dilemmas especially in the age of divorce. The list of questions about everyday etiquette is long and varied.

In a world that is increasingly informal and fast-paced, etiquette's guidelines have evolved to accommodate these changes. New customs have emerged—such as those involving modes of communications, like e-mail, cellular phones, fax machines, and the Internet. Yet even in this fast-changing world, I find that simple courtesies have a place. Whether you're communicating the old-fashioned way, by letter or telephone, or electronically, via e-mail, I say that kindness and consideration for others are the best guides. As my great-grandmother-in-law Emily Post once said, "Acts of kindness make our world a pleasanter place to live."

Emily Post taught me that the essence of etiquette is not one of adherence to strict rules and antiquated customs but of consideration for others. I define good manners as simply incorporating kindness and thoughtfulness for others into the fabric of our everyday lives. Etiquette has changed very little: Many things that were important in Emily Post's day are still relevant. Thanking a donor promptly and graciously for a gift, for example. Helping friends in need, or making guests feel comfortable and welcome at a party are as important today as in years past.

To that end, I've filled this handy pocket guide with practical at-a-glance answers to more than 250 of the most-asked etiquette questions of modern life. *Emily Post's Essentials: Everyday Etiquette* offers solutions to the often sticky situations we face every day—such as:

- When to send invitations by e-mail
- How to get along with the mother of your stepchildren
- What to say to a friend who's been downsized from her job
- How to respond to nosy questions about when you're planning to start a family
- Whether it's correct to change a baby's diaper in public
- The proper wedding seating and receiving-line order when parents are divorced

I've found that, far from being stuffy and constraining, manners are simply the tools we use to get along with others in an increasingly complicated world. *Everyday Etiquette* offers practical solutions to the most common etiquette questions of everyday life. Let it be your guide to maintaining the little courtesies that add up to make the world a more pleasant place to live.

—*Peggy Post*
March 1999

CHAPTER 1

GREETINGS AND INTRODUCTIONS

Q. *What are the traditional rules for making introductions? Are there forms that should be avoided?*

A. The overall guideline is that one person is introduced to another. This is achieved either by the actual use of the word "to"—"Mr. Benson, I'd like to introduce you to Mr. Smith"—or by saying the name of the person to whom the other is being introduced first, without using the preposition "to." An example of this is: "Mrs. Newgaard, may I introduce Mr. Collier."

In addition to the overall rule, there are three basic guidelines:

1. **In social situations, a man is generally introduced to a woman.** "Mrs. Pullman, I'd like you to meet Mr. Havlin." "Janny, this is my cousin, Sid Vaccaro." "Mr. DeRuvo, may I introduce you to my mother, Mrs. Smithson." In business situations, the man–woman combination is replaced by the next guideline about prominence or importance.

2. **A less prominent person is always introduced to a more prominent person.** This rule can be complicated, since it may be difficult to determine

who is more prominent. There is one guideline that may help in some circumstances: Members of your family, even though they may be more prominent, are introduced to the other person as a matter of courtesy.

"Mr. Connor, I'd like you to meet my stepfather, Governor Bradley."

"Mrs. Anselmi, this is my aunt, Professor Johnston."

3. **A young person is always introduced to an older person.**

"Dr. Josephson, I'd like you to meet my daughter, Lily Peterson."

"Aunt Ruth, this is my roommate, Elizabeth Feeney."

The easiest way not to slip up is to always say the name of the woman, the older person, or the more prominent person first, followed by the phrase, "I'd like you to meet . . ." or "this is . . ." or "may I introduce . . ." If you inadvertently say the wrong name first, correct your slip by saying, "Mr. Heath, I'd like to introduce you to Mrs. McGregor."

The following are forms to be avoided:

- Don't introduce people by their first names only. Always include a person's full name.
- When phrasing your introduction, avoid expressing it as a command, such as, "Mr. Bonner, shake hands with Mr. Heath," or "Mrs. Digby, meet my cousin, Barbara."

- Try to avoid calling only one person "my friend" in an introduction. It can imply that the other person isn't your friend.
- When introducing yourself, don't begin by saying, "What's your name?" Start by giving your own name: "Hello, I'm Joan Hamburg . . ."
- Do not repeat "Mr. Jones...Mr. Smith. Mr. Smith... Mr. Jones." To say each name once is enough.
- Do not refer to your spouse as "Mr. Jansen" or "Mrs. J." in conversation. Rather, refer to him or her as "my husband" or "my wife" in situations where first names are not being used.

Q. *Are there occasions when first names aren't used? What are they?*

A. Yes, there are. When meeting one of the following people, first names may not be used except when they request it:

- A superior in one's business.
- A business client or customer.
- A person of higher rank (a diplomat, a public official, a professor, for example).
- Professional people offering you their services (doctors, lawyers, etc.). In turn, they should not use your first name unless you request them to.
- An older person.

Q. *Is it necessary to specify my relationship to someone when introducing family members?*

A. No, it is not necessary, but it is helpful to include an identifying phrase. This provides a conversational opening for strangers. Since you courteously give precedence to the other person when introducing a family member, the identifying phrase comes at the end of the introduction: "Mrs. Cottrell, I'd like you to meet my daughter, Deborah."

Q. *How do you introduce a live-in partner?*

A. Although you usually identify family members as such, you needn't identify boyfriends, girlfriends, or live-in companions with their relationship to you. Saying his or her name is sufficient.

Q. *Should children introduce their parents by using first names?*

A. It depends on to whom they are making the introduction. One should always use the name that the newly introduced pair will use in talking to each other. If you are introducing your roommate to your father, he would, of course, call your father by the title "Mr." If you are introducing your roommate's father to your father, you would use your father's full name: "Mr. Davies, may I introduce my father, Franklin Palmer."

Q. *How should stepparents be introduced?*

A. There is nothing derogatory or objectionable in the

terms stepmother or stepfather, and the simplest form of introduction, said in the warmest tone to indicate an affectionate relationship, is: "Mrs. Hibbing, I'd like you to meet my stepfather, Mr. Brown." Even if you call your stepfather by his first name, he should be introduced to your peers or younger persons as "Mr. Brown," not "Jack."

Q. *How should ex-family members be introduced?*

A. If the introduction is very casual and it is not likely that any of the people involved will see each other again, no explanation is necessary. If the new acquaintanceship is likely to continue, it is important to explain the relationship as clearly as possible. A former mother-in-law would say, "I'd like you to meet Mary Dunbar. Mary is John's (or my son's) widow and is now married to Joe Dunbar." Had Mary been divorced, the mother-in-law would say, "Mary was John's wife and is now married to . . ." Mary's introduction of her former mother-in-law will be, "This is Mrs. Judson, Sarah's grandmother," or "my first husband's mother."

Q. *How are professional women introduced in social situations?*

A. They are introduced by stating their first and last names. If a woman has a specific title, it should be added. If, for example, a woman is a medical doctor, she is introduced with her title, socially as well as professionally.

Q. *I often forget people's names and am at a loss to introduce them to others. How can I make introductions under these situations?*

A. One thing you can do is to introduce the friend who has joined you to the person whose name you've forgotten by saying to the latter, "Oh, do you know Janet McCall?" Hopefully the nameless person will be tactful and understanding enough to announce his own name. If he doesn't, and your friend makes matters worse by saying, "You didn't tell me his name," it can be even more embarrassing. Your other approach is to be completely frank, admit you're having a mental block, and ask the person to complete the introduction themselves.

Remember the feeling, however, when you meet someone who obviously doesn't remember your name. Offer it at once. Say immediately, "Hello, I'm Julie Hopewell. I met you at the Andersons' last Christmas." Never say, "You don't remember me, do you?" which only serves to embarrass the other person.

Q. *What can I say when introduced besides, "How do you do?"*

A. Whether you say "how do you do" or "hello" when introduced to another, follow with the person's name, which helps commit the name to memory. Your tone of voice indicates degrees of warmth, and if you are introduced to someone you have wanted to meet, you can follow "How do you do, Mr. Struthers" or "Hello, Mrs. Jenson" with "I'm so glad to meet you—Jerry Ernst speaks of you all the time!" or whatever may be the reason for your special interest.

Q. *How do I correct my host or hostess when I've been incorrectly introduced?*

A. It is sensible and kind to correct the error immediately, but never with annoyance. Make light of it, if possible, so you don't embarrass the host or hostess. All you need to say is, "Actually, it's Tracey, not Stacey—people get it confused all the time!"

Q. *My name is a little unusual and frequently mispronounced. My new next-door neighbor has said it incorrectly for several months, to the point that it would embarrass her if I corrected her now. What should I do?*

A. You can explain the situation to a mutual friend and ask her to correct your neighbor at a suitable time. If your neighbor apologizes, tell her not to think anything of it. Or, if you think correcting her directly would only embarrass her, you could nonetheless comment as diplomatically as possible, something along the lines of: "My name is pretty unusual and easy to mispronounce. Don't feel bad—many people have trouble saying it. It's _____, not _____."

Q. *What name does a divorced woman use?*

A. A divorced woman does not continue to use her husband's first name and so is addressed as Mrs. (or Ms.) Margaret Thune, not Mrs. Andrew Thune—unless she decides to revert to the use of her maiden name.

Q. *Does a married woman's name differ from the form a widow uses?*

A. No. Traditionally, a woman who is currently married and a widow generally use the same form, "Mrs. George Yost." Today, many married women and some widows prefer to use their first name instead of their husband's. Many older women prefer to continue using their husband's name, however. When in doubt about addressing a woman of any age, either err on the side of tradition or ask her which form she prefers.

Q. *I never know whether or not to shake hands. Are there any guidelines to help me judge this situation?*

A. Yes, there are guidelines, but they are flexible. Strictly speaking, from a traditional standpoint, in a social situation it is a woman's place to offer her hand or not to a man. But if he should extend his hand first, she should give him hers. Technically, it has been the place of a man to whom another is being introduced to offer his hand first, but the gesture is usually simultaneous.

Adults offer their hands to children first. If you think about it, the guidelines for shaking hands follow the guidelines for introductions: A woman offers her hand first; an older person initiates a handshake with a younger one; and the more important person, or the one to whom someone is being introduced, is the first to offer his or her hand.

Q. *Under what circumstances does a man rise when introduced to a woman? Do women stand when being introduced? Does it matter if the situation is social or for business?*

A. There is a variation between social and business settings. In a social situation, a man should rise when a woman comes into a room for the first time and remain standing until she is seated or leaves the vicinity, or unless she says, "Thank you, but please sit down," or words to that effect. The man does not jump up and down every time a hostess or another guest goes in and out of the room.

When a client goes to a man's office on business, he should stand up and receive the client, offer a chair, and wait until the client is seated—whether the client is a man or a woman. When the client rises to leave, he should stand, escort the client to the door, and hold the door for him or her. Neither man nor woman rises for a secretary or office coworker.

A woman receiving a male client in her office generally follows the same guidelines as given above for a man receiving clients in his office. Although she might remain seated if the client were a much younger person, she would definitely rise for a much older woman.

In a restaurant, when a woman greets a man in passing, he merely makes the gesture of rising slightly from his chair and nodding. If she pauses to speak for a moment, he rises fully and introduces her to others at his table.

Both the host and hostess always rise to greet each arriving guest. Members of the host's family, including young people, also rise as a guest enters the room, with the exception of a child who is sitting and chatting with an adult. He or she may continue the conversation, seated, unless the guest is brought over to be introduced, in which case the child should rise.

A woman does not stand when being introduced to someone at a distance, nor need she rise when shaking hands with anyone, unless the person is much older, very prominent, or is someone with whom she wants to go on talking. A woman should not jump to her feet for a woman who is only a few years older than herself, since rising indicates, among other things, respect for age. The gesture, although well meant, would more than likely not be well received.

CHAPTER 2

THE ART OF CONVERSATION

Q. *I'm often at a loss when starting a conversation with a stranger. Can you give me any hints on how to get the conversation going?*

A. Learn the art of being a good listener—don't monopolize the conversation. It's been said that "I" is the smallest letter in the alphabet. Don't make it the largest word in your vocabulary. Take your turn. Describe something you have been doing or an interesting article you have read, then stop and ask your new acquaintance his opinion about or experiences with the topic. People tend to be responsive when you ask their advice or opinion. Finally, don't panic over a period of silence—you needn't try to fill it by chattering aimlessly.

Q. *How can I answer tacky personal questions? I'm always at a loss on how to respond to nosy questions regarding such issues as my age or the cost of a gift or outfit.*

A. If you are asked your age and don't care to divulge it, you simply don't have to. You might say, "Old enough to know better" or "Thirty-nine and holding."

Neither are you under any obligation to answer a query about the cost of a gift or the price of something you are wearing. You can either plead ignorance, saying you can't recall, or you can say, "I'd rather not talk about that, if you don't mind. With the cost of living what it is, the whole subject is too depressing . . ." and change the subject.

Q. *What is the best way to talk to a deaf or hearing-impaired person?*

A. There are many degrees of hearing impairment, from partial loss of hearing in one ear to complete deafness. If you know that the hearing loss is in one ear, it is considerate to sit on the side of the good ear when it isn't possible to sit face to face. In the case of total hearing loss, the only means of communication is visual, through lip-reading or sign language.

When talking, speak slowly and distinctly. Turn toward him when you speak. Be patient while talking and willing to repeat or rephrase.

Always include him in conversation, making sure he can see you or the group—and make sure others also speak directly to him. Encourage family and friends to be more inclusive and aware; persons with severe disabilities tend to withdraw into themselves because their handicap isolates them.

Q. *When I meet blind people I sometimes find myself speaking more loudly, probably because I don't really know what to do and am uncomfortable in their presence. How should I act?*

A. Keep in mind that in every other respect blind people are probably much like you. Blind people's other faculties are in no way impaired because of their blindness and may be more sensitively developed to compensate for their loss of sight. It's a common mistake, in talking with a blind person, to speak louder than usual. Use a normal voice; hearing impairment is not his handicap.

It is correct to ask a blind person if you can help him cross the street, but never grasp his arm or try to give assistance without first asking whether you may. Let the blind person take your arm rather than your propelling him or her. When walking with a blind person, mention any upcoming obstacles, a step, for instance, or a corner to be turned. If the blind person has a guide dog, do not attempt to play with or distract the dog in any way. Its attention must remain fully on its master, whose safety and well-being depends on the dog's strict adherence to its training. Finally, don't avoid the use of the word *see*. A blind person uses it as much as anyone else.

Q. *Two friends and I were having lunch when one of them turned to the other and whispered something in her ear. I thought this was rude and felt offended. What is your opinion?*

A. I agree with you. It is very rude to whisper in front of other people. If you know the offenders fairly well, you could have pointed out their slight by lightly saying, "Hey, you two! Don't you know you're leaving me out?" Hopefully, they would have realized their rudeness and stopped.

Q. *A new friend of mine is Protestant. I am Jewish. I know little about his faith and am embarrassed about expressing my ignorance. Plus, I don't want to offend him by asking him about something he may consider private. Would it be inappropriate to ask him to explain it to me?*

A. It would be fine. If he practices his faith it is important to him, and you are being both polite and thoughtful in asking him to talk about something that is meaningful to his life. While your new friend initially may not feel comfortable sharing his innermost spiritual thoughts with you, he would probably be happy to explain the basic tenets of his religion.

Q. *What is the appropriate response when people tell you that they have cancer or AIDS or some terminal disease? I never know what to say.*

A. Simply say that you are sorry to hear it, ask them how they're doing, and ask if there is anything you can do. Tell them you appreciate their telling you. Make an effort to reply in a compassionate, interested tone, and listen attentively to them.

Q. *I am a large woman and proud of it. How do I handle such rude comments as "When is the baby due?" or "You obviously have a healthy appetite."*

A. Such comments are thoughtless at best and incredibly rude at worst. You can simply be direct. Without getting angry, calmly tell them that you don't appreciate their comment, that you find it inconsiderate and inappropriate.

Q. *How do I talk to people at a party where I know no one?*

A. Going to a party alone and knowing no one can test even the most confident and self-assured among us. Swallow, take a deep breath, and step into the fray and introduce yourself. Say something like, "Hi, I'm Jim Gray; do you mind if I join you?" Find your host, who should have the wherewithal to introduce you to others. Make small talk with people when standing at the bar or around the food table. You can always comment on the food to get the ball rolling.

Q. *My good friend has recently converted to a new religion. I find that much of our conversation revolves around converting me as well. I have no interest in doing so; how can I tell my friend to drop the subject without being rude?*

A. Be honest; tell your friend you are happy that he has found spiritual meaning in his life, but that you are content as you are. Tell him that his proselytizing is making you uncomfortable, and that while you appreciate the interest he has in your well-being, you're concerned that his behavior could harm the friendship you share.

CHAPTER 3

TELEPHONES, COMPUTERS, AND LETTERS

Q. *What is the proper way to answer the telephone?*

A. The best way to answer the telephone at home is still "Hello." There is no need to identify yourself when answering your home telephone.

Q. *Does a caller give his or her name as soon as the phone is answered?*

A. Yes. Not only is it courteous, but it is helpful as well.

- To an adult you say: "This is Helen Franklin. Is Nancy Henry in?"
- To a child you say: "This is Mrs. Franklin. Is your mother in?"
- When you recognize the voice, say: "Hello, John. This is Helen. Is Sue there?"
- When the person you are calling answers, say: "Hi, Sue. This is Helen," or, "Hello, Mrs. Brooks. This is Helen Franklin."
- A young person calling an older man or woman says: "Hello, Mrs. Knox. This is Janet Frost."

- A young child calling a friend says: "Hello, Mrs. Knox. This is Janet Frost. May I please speak to Tammy?"

If a caller does not identify herself, it is correct to ask who is calling, even though it can be a little awkward. The recipient of the call has a better chance of being prepared to talk if the caller's identity is known upfront. It is also a matter of safety to inquire as to the identity of the caller. Many calls are made just to find out whether a house is empty, or whether there is an adult at home. If a child—or an adult—answering doesn't recognize the voice of the caller, he or she should say, "Who is calling, please?" If the name is unfamiliar and the caller does not further identify herself, a child should be taught not to say, "He's not home now." Instead he should say, "He's busy just now," or "He's not available just now—may he return your call?"

Q. *How do you respond to an invitation made by phone? Must you give an immediate response?*

A. It is incumbent on the person calling to explain the invitation right up front. You're putting someone on the spot if you start out the conversation with "What are you doing Saturday night?" or "Are you busy Sunday afternoon?" without explaining why you want to know.

Therefore, if the caller does not have the courtesy to explain the invitation, but asks only, "Are you busy

Saturday night?" you may say, "I don't know if John has made any commitments for Saturday—I'll check with him. Why do you ask?" This forces the caller to issue a proper invitation.

When a telephone invitation is issued, it is rude to respond with "I'll let you know," unless it is immediately followed by an explanation, such as checking with a spouse for previous commitments or the like. Without this, "I'll let you know" sounds as though you are waiting for a better invitation to come along.

Q. *How do you handle a wrong-number call?*

A. If you are the person who has dialed a wrong number, don't ask, "What number is this?" Ask instead, "Is this 555-0451?" so that you can look the number up or dial more carefully.

When you are the recipient of a wrong-number call, don't give out your number to the caller. Simply inform him or her politely that he has dialed the wrong number.

Q. *What is the best way to handle obscene calls?*

A. Hang up immediately. Don't give the caller the satisfaction of hearing you become upset or even responding. If, as sometimes happens, the call is repeated as soon as you hang up, leave the receiver off the hook for a little while.

If you are subjected to such calls regularly, consider having a caller I.D. installed that can show the number of the person calling.

There is another remedy you can use to discourage the occasional obscene caller. Keep an ordinary police whistle by the phone, and as soon as you hear the first obscene word, blow a hard blast right into the telephone speaker. Not only should that discourage future phone calls, but it should also give you a sense of empowerment.

Q. *Are business telephone manners different from social telephone manners?*

A. Yes, business telephone manners differ from at-home telephone manners in several ways. When answering a business call, an assistant or secretary gives his or her supervisor's name: "Miss Moore's office (or Roz Moore's office). May I help you?" If people answer their phones directly, they usually identify themselves: "Hello, this is Roz Moore" or simply, "Roz Moore."

The caller identifies himself in this case, as with a personal or social call: "Hello. This is Tom Price. Is Miss Moore in?" or "Hello, Miss Moore. This is Tom Price. I'm with the Brownstone Company."

As with an at-home call, it is correct to ask the caller: "May I ask who is calling, please?" if he fails to identify himself. In some offices, a secretary or assistant may also ask, "May I ask what this call is in reference to?" or less bluntly, "Will Miss Moore know what this call is about?"

Although it is not courteous to tie up a telephone line for long at home, it is particularly to be avoided in the office. Long personal conversations are not only out of place, but also wasteful of the time that belongs to the company, not to the employee.

Q. *When I visit a friend, she will answer the telephone and chat with the caller for ten or fifteen minutes. I think this is rude. If the call is a long distance one or one relaying pertinent information, I can understand staying on the line. But when it is a local call and the conversation is basic chit-chat, I feel she should tell the caller she is busy and ask if she can call back. Am I wrong?*

A. No, you are not wrong. No one should carry on an extended phone call when she has a visitor.

Q. *I'm getting fed up with calling someone and then being put on hold while she takes another call. Is there some guideline for using call waiting?*

A. The only way to handle call waiting with any kind of courtesy is to handle the process quickly and kindly. Excuse yourself briefly from your first call, answer the second call, take the number, and return immediately to the original call. When you are waiting for a call, or when members of your household are out and you think they may be calling for a ride or for help, you should say so at the beginning of a call with another person. Your friend may decide to call back later, or ask you to call her at a more convenient time.

Q. *I utilize a telephone service that enables me to forward my calls to another number. Sometimes it is important for me to do this; when my children are out, for example, and might need assistance, or when I am waiting for an overseas call that is late and I have to go on to another appointment. Is it an intrusion on someone else to forward my calls to their number?*

A. Yes, it is if you fail to discuss the necessity of fowarding your calls. The best way to handle this is to call the person to whose number you would like to forward your calls and ask if it is all right. Explain why, and mention that there may be a few extraneous calls that come along with the one you are waiting for that will be a bother to her until you can get home again to disable the call forwarding function. If she doesn't mind, then it is a good idea to give her the gist of your message or questions in case the call comes between the time you put your telephone on forwarding and travel to her house or office.

Q. *I take the train to work and am disturbed at the rudeness of cellphone users who chat away loudly and constantly. Would it be equally rude of me to ask them to curtail their phone-calling or at least try to do it more quietly?*

A. The commuter who talks away on call after call earns the ire of all around him, and justifiably so. Why? Because he or she is, in effect, invading private space in close quarters. A considerate businessperson knows that all but the most urgent calls should be made from the office as a matter of course. And what about the ringing phones at sporting events, concerts, and movie screenings? They're *all* intrusions. It is certainly correct to politely ask that a cellphone owner turn off or turn down the ringer, or try to talk more quietly.

Q. *I get annoyed at people who don't return phone calls. What are some general guidelines for returning phone calls?*

A. Not calling back is the equivalent of standing someone up. Make an effort to return calls left on your answering machine or voice mail within twenty-four hours. If you reach a machine, lessen the potential for "telephone tag" by stating where you can be reached and when.

Q. *Is it proper to send notes via the fax to friends?*

A. Sure, especially to someone who has a fax machine in his or her home, which makes it a fairly private means of communication. In an office, where the equipment is usually located at a central point, transmittals can be read by anyone who happens to be walking by the machine. And, personal faxes sent to an office can interfere with the receipt of work-related faxes and should thus be avoided.

Q. *My penmanship isn't very good. May I type my personal letters?*

A. Yes, it is absolutely correct to type a personal letter if writing is difficult. As more and more of us have computers and printers capable of producing lovely script your personal correspondence needn't look like a business letter anymore. For those with legible penmanship, however, the warmth of a hand-written note is still preferable—especially for condolence notes and thank-you notes that are not part of longer letters.

Q. *How do you address correspondence to a married couple who use different surnames? Would the form of address differ if they were not married?*

A. Correspondence to a married couple with different names should be addressed so that both names appear on the same line:

> **Mr. Jonathan Adams and Ms. Angela Blake**

If the couple is unmarried, the names should be on separate lines:

> **Ms. Susan Amber**
> **Mr. Howard Cole**

Q. *How should a married woman sign letters, with her business name or married name? Does it matter if the letter is for business or social purposes?*

A. If a woman continues to use her own name in business after marriage, she would sign business correspondence with her maiden name. If she uses her husband's name socially, her personal correspondence would be signed with her first name (and married name if the recipient needs it for identification purposes). If a woman uses her own name both in business and socially, all correspondence would be signed with her own name.

Q. *How is an envelope addressed to a couple when the woman uses her maiden name as part of her name?*

A. Most women do keep their maiden name as a middle name, but it is not ordinarily used when you are addressing an envelope to her and her husband, as a couple. She uses it in her signature—"Mary Field Smith"—and she may use it professionally. Letters to the couple are simply addressed to "Mr. and Mrs. John Smith." If she is hyphenating the two names, however, then the mail is addressed to "Ms. Mary Field-Smith and Mr. John Smith." It's also acceptable to write his name first, hers second.

Q. *What is the proper salutation at the beginning of a letter when you do not know the name and/or gender* *of the person to whom you are writing?*

A. "Dear Sir or Madam" is the best solution when you are writing to a person whose name and/or gender you do not know. Other options are to use the salutation "To Whom It May Concern" or to call the establishment to ascertain the name of the recipient of your correspondence.

Q. *How is a letter addressed to a couple when the woman is a Dr. and her husband is a Mr.?*

A. You would write to "Dr. Lynn and Mr. Marc Josephson." If she kept her maiden name professionally, you would write to "Dr. Lynn Finnigan and Mr. Mark Josephson."

Q. *We have friends who are both dentists. How do we address their cards?*

A. Letters to them should be addressed "Dr. Cynthia and Dr. James Haven" or to "Drs. Cynthia and James Haven."

Q. *We have a woman pastor at our church. What is the proper way to address mail to her and her husband?*

A. The proper form is "The Reverend Joan and Mr. John Smith."

Q. *My husband is a psychologist and he worked hard to earn the title "Dr." However, I believe it is not proper for him to sign his name Dr. Doe when he signs the restaurant bill or another credit card slip. Am I correct?*

A. Your husband should not sign his name "Dr. John Doe" just as another man does not sign "Mr. William Smith." He should be addressed as Dr., but his signature is simply "John Doe." To register in a hotel he signs "John Doe" unless you accompany him, in which case he would sign "Dr. and Mrs. John Doe."

Q. *What is the best way to address a letter to a male child? Is it Master to a certain age and then Mr.?*

A. Traditionally, children were addressed as "Master" until they were about six years old. Today "Master" is seen less often. No title is used until boys graduate from college or are in their early twenties, at which time they become "Mr."

Q. *May I include my children's names on our Christmas card, even though they both have their own apartments? I know they won't be sending cards to some of our old family friends and thought this was a way to extend a greeting from them.*

A. Ordinarily you do not sign for people not living under your roof. An alternative would be to sign your name and your husband's, and add a note that your children asked to be remembered to the receiver.

Q. *How do you feel about people sending Christmas cards detailing deaths of family members, illnesses, job losses, financial disasters, etc.? Three Christmases have been shadowed for me by cards from a college friend describing her progress with cancer. Surely a letter concerning these matters, if urgent, could be sent in November or January?*

A. I agree. Christmas cards should be messages of faith, hope, and joy. They should not be used to purvey all of the terrible news that one wishes to impart. That should be done in a separate message, preferably sent after Christmas when the sad tidings will not destroy the joy of the Christmas season.

Q. *Is it proper to send printed Christmas cards to family and friends? I have read that if you don't want to bother to sign your name, it is better to send no card at all. What do you think?*

A. Printed Christmas cards are perfectly acceptable as long as you add a personal note on those sent to friends and family. When Christmas cards are sent to business associates, it is not necessary to add to the printed signature.

Q. *Sometimes there are occasions when I send greeting cards to immediate neighbors. Often, I place them in a* *door newspaper box or the mailbox, but I wonder if they should be mailed instead?*

A. There is nothing wrong with slipping a card under a neighbor's door or placing it in the newspaper box. However, it is against U.S. Postal Service regulations to place unstamped mail in a mailbox—so don't deliver your cards that way.

Q. *Over the years I have received several chain letters. Each one says that if I don't answer, I will disappoint everyone or have something terrible happen to me. The letters are usually from very good friends. I mind not only complying, but also inconveniencing six or more of my friends to continue the letter. What may I tactfully tell my friends when they ask why I haven't answered the letters?*

A. You are not alone in resenting chain letters. Most people find them an imposition. They invariably try to make you feel guilty if you break the chain and usually they fall far short of their promise. The best way to handle it is to return the letter to the sender with a short note: "Sorry, just don't have time . . . etc." and he can then send it to someone else if he wishes to keep his chain going.

Q. *My family has chosen to shorten our very long surname to a more manageable one. How can we let everyone know we've done this?*

A. The quickest and simplest way is to send out formal announcements:

> Mr. and Mrs. Brian Malinowsky
> Announce that by Permission of the Court
> They and Their Children
> Have Taken the Family Name of
> Malin

Q. *What form should a business e-mail letter follow?*

A. E-mail transmittals should follow the format of standard business letters. They should be succinct and professional; check for correct grammar and spelling, as well as neatness. When e-mailing someone's office computer, remember that the e-mail message you send is not necessarily confidential or private.

Q. *Every night we get at least two telephone solicitations. My husband has started hanging up on the callers. I think this is rude, because they are just doing their job, but I resent their intrusion, too. What's the best way to get off the phone without being rude?*

A. Simply and quickly say that you are not interested, thank you, and hang up. I agree that being rude to telemarketers is an unsatisfactory way to deal with the situation. It isn't necessary either to go the other extreme and keep them on the line if you know you're not interested. Doing so only wastes their time.

Q. *For what types of occasions is it acceptable to use computerized messages, or e-mail?*

A. E-mail has become so engrained in our culture that it is now being used to relay correspondence for many different types of occasions. Some people feel that it is acceptable to use e-mail for any occasion. While many people feel that the warmth of hand-written thank-yous are preferable to electronic ones, there are some circumstances in which an e-mail thank-you is fine—such as if the computer is the only way friends can communicate, or if it's part of a longer message. Informal party invitations are fine, but I draw the line at formal wedding invitations, formal dinner-party invitations, and condolence notes that are relayed by e-mail.

CHAPTER 4

MODERN DAILY LIFE

Q. *My ex-husband and I live in the same town. Our son lives with me, but his stepmother, who has children from a previous marriage, is involved in the same school activities. Her children use their father's last name, while her last name is the same as my son's and mine. How do we avoid confusion?*

A. There is no way to avoid confusion except by explaining. Eventually, people will figure out who's who. When someone unfamiliar with your situation gets confused, simply say, "Timmy is my son. His father is now married to Sally Anderson. Her children are Janet and Jackie Smith."

Q. *I have been married for less than a year. My husband has a fourteen-year-old son from a previous marriage. I think we have established a good relationship. He has a mother who lives nearby. I'm not sure what my role is supposed to be with her. We do meet every so often. Do you have any advice?*

A. Good manners dictate that you are at least civil and polite, at most friendly. Good sense dictates that you don't discuss the state of your marriage. As for your stepson, don't give unsolicited advice, although you could suggest to help, offering to drive him to dental appointments, say, or help him pick out some school clothes. If your stepson lives with his mother most of the time, you can ask her advice about when he visits with you. Questions about his regular bedtime, a curfew she has established, medical care, or other things having to do with her house rules would only reassure her that you respect her philosophy and are seeking to support it. Naturally, you would share any discussions of this nature with your husband.

Q. *It has been a long time since I have been on a date. Now that I am a single woman again, I need a refresher course on who pays for what, or whether I should just pay my own way, and on whether I can issue an invitation or must wait to be asked.*

A. Fortunately, dating etiquette has changed. Women don't have to sit by the phone hoping someone will call, and men don't have to carry the entire financial burden. When two people meet and sense that they would like to spend more time together, either may initiate a date. As to who pays, the guidelines are the same as they would be for two friends of the same gender. When an invitation is worded, "Would you have dinner with me on Saturday night?" the person inviting expects to pay, whether male or female. When two people decide, jointly, to buy tickets to an event or to meet for a meal, each would pay his or her own way, unless one insists on the other being his or her guest. If a relationship develops and one feels that the other is paying most of the costs of their dates, he or she should initiate plans and firmly say, "This evening is my treat," or, "I'd love to go, but I'll pick up the tickets this time."

Q. *These days, when walking down the street, are men expected to walk closest to the curb or to the buildings?*

A. The practice of men walking nearer the curb began as a way to protect women from runaway or obstreperous horses and splashing mud from carriage wheels on unpaved roads. Although the reason no longer exists, the pattern is still followed. If a man chooses to ignore the curbside rule, he should always walk on the woman's left.

Q. *Does the "ladies first" rule still apply?*

A. In many social situations, yes, if those involved are comfortable with the rule. However, many women today prefer no special treatment. This is fine, and it's their call. If a woman does not want to be "first," she can *graciously* say so. She should not get annoyed about a man's efforts to be courteous. She can make her modern viewpoint known by kindly telling him that she doesn't follow the "ladies first" tradition. Then, she can take turns with him by sometimes saying, "Thanks, but you go first."

In most social circumstances, indoors or out, a

couple walks side by side. When it's necessary to walk single file, the woman precedes the man (to follow a waiter to a table, for instance). There are times, however, when traditionally a man goes first. The following list describes such situations:

- Over rough ground, the man walks beside the woman and offers his hand if she needs assistance.
- He steps ahead of her to open a car door for her to enter.
- He gets out of a car first and holds the door for her when they arrive, unless she doesn't want to wait.
- He precedes her down a steep or slippery stairway. However, he follows her up or down an escalator unless she asks him to go first to help her on or off.
- He makes the gesture of stepping into a boat first, or off a bus first, to be ready to help her, unless she prefers that he not do so.
- He steps into a revolving door that is not already moving ahead of a woman, but she precedes him through one that is already moving.

Q. *Are men still expected to give up their seats for women on trains and buses? What about children giving up seats to adults?*

A. A man is not expected to give up his seat unless a woman is elderly, infirm, pregnant, or burdened with a baby or a heavy armful of any sort. Otherwise it is to be assumed that a man who has worked all day is just as tired as the women on the train or bus. Of course a man may offer his seat to any woman if he wishes, and she may accept or graciously refuse his offer as she wishes. Children, on the other hand, should be taught to offer their seats to older people, both men and women. Generally, youngsters are strong, they have not usually worked as hard during the day, and furthermore, it is a gesture of courtesy and respect.

Q. *Who gets off the elevator first, men or women?*

A. In a crowded elevator, whoever is nearest the door gets off first, whether man or woman. In elevators that are not crowded or apartment or private elevators, a woman may precede a man out the door, if he offers and she wants to accept this traditional courtesy.

Q. *Are there any acceptable public displays of affection, such as walking hand in hand down the street?*

A. There is nothing wrong with walking hand in hand in public, unless doing so causes pedestrian traffic to be impeded. In this case, single file is the rule until the sidewalk is less crowded. Acceptable forms of public displays of affection are holding hands, and casual or affectionate kisses or hugs when greeting or saying good-bye. Other physical displays of affection should take place in private.

Q. *Since my divorce I have begun dating a woman who seems interested in establishing a physical relationship. I am concerned about AIDS and other sexually transmitted diseases. How do I discuss this without offending her?*

A. It is very difficult and extremely embarrassing to most people to ask, "What have you been doing, with whom, and when?" My opinion is that if you are willing to bare all with someone else, you should also be able to bare your thoughts. Some sexually transmitted diseases (STDs) have cures. Others do not. A moment of passion, no matter how blissful, is not worth the ending of your life, prematurely and painfully. With someone you have only recently met, there is absolutely nothing wrong with saying, "I'm sorry, but until we know each other better and feel more comfortable talking about sex, we just can't get involved in a sexual relationship. There is too much at risk." If she or he becomes insulted, so be it. With someone with whom you are considering establishing a long-term relationship, you must talk openly. Never name names, but if you or your partner has had an active sex life, it is only fair to the other to have or to request a blood and medical checkup to make sure you are healthy and not carrying disease. Because people have been known to lie about the results of such tests, it is not out of line for you to insist that you exchange results before entering into any intimate relationship. And, while condoms are not a guaranteed protection against disease, a woman has every right to insist that her partner wear one. Never throw precaution to the wind just to avoid insulting a sexual partner.

Q. *Can you offer any guidelines for apartment living?*

A. The best guideline, as with many rules of etiquette, is the consideration of others. Don't do things you wouldn't want done to you. Don't deface property, litter, allow garbage to build up, or be insensitive about noise. Children's play may not seem loud, nor does the radio, stereo, or television set when you're in the same room with them, but those sounds carry easily from one apartment to another. Although some noise is to be expected, it is not to be expected at the crack of dawn or late at night. At these times, noisemaking should be eliminated. You may soften the noise in your apartment by requesting your landlord install double-paned windows, putting down carpet, or building bookshelves.

Q. *My town does not have a law regarding picking up after a dog. Many dog-walkers do this anyway, but there is one person in my neighborhood who walks her dog past my house every day. Without fail, he stops and uses my front yard. I then have to scoop up what he has left behind. Should I say anything?*

A. Yes. The next time you see them coming, walk out to greet them. Simply say that you enjoy seeing them walk by and understand that the dog needs to "go," but that since he frequently selects your yard as a rest stop, you find yourself cleaning up after him regularly. Say that you don't enjoy this, and ask that the neighbor please pick up after her dog. You can then ask a friendly question, such as the dog's name, or how old the dog is, chat a moment, and say farewell. If you find that this neighbor disregards your reasonable request, then you should continue to make it until she is so embarrassed that she takes a different route, or until she learns to clean up after her own dog.

Q. *I try to volunteer as much as possible in my community. A few times, I have been teamed with others who do not do their own share of the work, leaving me to do it myself. Would it be rude to point this out?*

A. Yes, because it would serve no purpose. Doing so may even make it look like you are whining about how hard you worked, or as if you are seeking praise. If possible, be discriminating in the future about the persons with whom you share responsibilities. If one of those who dumped her work on you in the past indicates that she wants to work with you again, just say, "Oh, I'm sorry Molly, I'm already working with Janet."

Q. *My boyfriend and I live together. When we visit my parents, who know we live together, they always give us separate rooms. Is there any way we can suggest that we want to share a room?*

A. Certainly you may make the suggestion, but if they say no you must respect their wishes or stay elsewhere when visiting. It is, after all, their home, and their house rules apply.

Q. *My husband and I are having trouble conceiving, and the process has been a long and painful one. Friends and family keep asking us when we're going to start a family. How do we put a stop to the questions without being rude?*

A. However well-intentioned their motives, people who continually broach such a private subject are being rude and inconsiderate. Certainly close family members should be apprised of the situation, and can be of help in relaying to friends, without going into any details, that you and your spouse have not made a decision on starting a family. When people ask you, repeat that, or simply answer, "We don't know." If they persist, bluntly state that it's not a subject you're comfortable discussing at this time.

Q. *My husband and I are an older couple who started a family late in life. We get a lot of comments about our "grandchildren." Our children are too young to be bothered by this now, but we are afraid they will be embarrassed by this as they grow older. How do we let people know that these are our children without being rude?*

A. Older parents are no longer an uncommon phenomenon in society, and your children will undoubtedly grow up to be aware of this fact. Nonetheless, it's awkward and presumptuous for anyone—especially a stranger—to make a verbal assumption regarding your relationship with your children. One way to get around this is to block it before it happens; make it known loud and clear that you are the parents—say, "Give your pacifier to Mommy" or "Let Daddy help you put your coat on."

Q. *Road rage is a real problem in my community. I have to commute to work every day. How does one best handle an angry and aggressive driver?*

A. Don't let a driver who is recklessly aggressive, who cuts off other drivers, or who threatens others with rude, hostile behavior affect your own driving. The best thing you can do is stay away from an obviously hostile driver—and don't get into a driving duel, where muscling each other's cars in and out of traffic risks causing an accident.

Q. *Is it considered bad manners to change a baby's diaper in public these days?*

A. In most cases, yes. But sometimes getting to a public changing room is impossible. In this instance, the mother should find as discreet a spot as possible, such as on a park bench. If she is with someone else, that person could assist her by being a shield to curious stares.

Q. *I am a gay man in a monogamous relationship but prefer to keep my private life private at work. Office matchmakers are constantly trying to "fix me up" with single woman friends. I always turn them down, but they keep after me. What can I do?*

A. While well-intentioned, matchmaking can also be intrusive and meddling. You're right: Your private life *is* private. All you need to do is keep saying no. After enough refusals, even the most determined office matchmaker will throw in the towel.

Q. *I had a baby fifteen months ago and have returned back to work full-time. My husband also works full-time. We have hired a nanny to look after the baby during the day. Is is proper for me to ask her to do light housework as well?*

A. You may, if you've discussed doing so up front, before she was hired, or give her the option of increasing her job duties (and pay) if you've already agreed upon her responsibilities. She may only be interested in childcare—or she may be flexible enough to do some light cleaning during baby's naptimes. Talk it over with her.

Q. *I ran into a recently divorced friend at a cocktail party. Would it have been appropriate for me to have* *brought up the subject of her divorce? What about when a friend is involved in a potentially embarrassing incident, such as declaring bankruptcy or getting a ticket for driving under the influence of alcohol?*

A. Divorce can be one of life's most traumatic events, and not saying something to a good friend may be even be more awkward than bringing up the subject. Simply express your condolences, and let her know you are there to help her in any way possible. You should never use the occasion to bad-mouth a friend's ex-spouse.

If you find yourself in a social situation with a friend who has gone through a potentially embarrassing experience, unless you are a very close friend, it is best not to bring up the subject at all.

CHAPTER 5

BUSINESS LIFE

Q. *How important are manners at work? Isn't how well you do the job what is really important?*

A. Good manners are part of a job well done. Even if you work alone, there is often contact with others, whether a delivery person, the night custodian, or a store sales clerk. Being aware of and kind to others, the cornerstone of good manners, help make everyday interactions run smoothly. More than one executive has missed the opportunity for promotion by not rising to greet a visitor, by displaying shoddy mealtime manners, and even failing to make eye contact. Every member of a company should act as an ambassador of the organization. Bad manners are not just bad for the individual; they're bad for business.

Q. *I do a lot of local traveling with my boss. Sometimes we travel by taxi, but mostly we use the company car and driver. Am I supposed to sit in the front or the back? And what about open seating at business meetings? I'm often unsure about where I should sit.*

A. Use common sense—don't be the first to rush to

the car. Wait until your boss has chosen where he will sit, and then sit wherever there is room. There's a story about a young executive who lost his chance for promotion because he sat in the roomier front seat, leaving the CEO a spot in the backseat, already crowded by two other members of the firm. When traveling by taxi, the least preferred seat is next to the driver. Take that seat if you are traveling with those senior to you. If you are traveling in the company limousine and several are traveling together, it may be that the best seat is in the front, where there is more leg and elbow room. Defer to the senior members of the firm; let them choose their spot, and then take a seat yourself.

The same philosophy holds true at a meeting where there are no designated seats or name plates. You should wait to be told by a senior person where to sit. If no one gives you direction, ask. It may be that it doesn't matter. But if it does, and you accidentally take a senior partner's seat, you are setting yourself up for the embarrassment of being asked to move.

Q. *When starting a new job, how do I know if I should use first names or address people by title and last name?*

A. In most industries when you first meet people, it is safest to use a title—"Mr.," "Mrs.," or "Ms."—until such time as you are asked to do otherwise. In return you should suggest that they call you by your first name as well.

Q. *When my husband and I attend social functions for his company, he will kiss some of the female employees as well as his secretary as a "hello." Although this is a simple kiss on the cheek, I don't feel it is appropriate. Do you?*

A. Generally, no, although the answer depends upon the situation. Kissing has no place in business surroundings among people who barely know each other or people who see each other all the time. If your husband had been away for a time and was greeting his employees after an absence, he might be justified in giving them a kiss in a social situation, but when he is working with them regularly, there is no justification for that type of greeting—even socially.

Q. *There is a great deal of socializing in my company, in the form of weekend outings, dinner parties, and the like. Frankly, the hours I put in during the week are quite enough for me. I have a life outside of my office and resent the pressure to extend my weekdays through 'round-the-clock and weekend gatherings. I don't want to hurt my chances for promotion, but enough is enough! What should I do?*

A. You should hang on to your priorities. It is not uncommon for business to occupy much, if not most, of our leisure time. Your home life, family, and outside interests should certainly be at least as important as your career. It is also important to have friends and community involvement outside of your job, interests that remain should you lose your job or retire. For many years there was no question that business socializing was part of the path to success. Today an employee may feel pressured to narrow his or her life to the job and coworkers. However, dedication to one's responsibilities, being able to say, every day, "that was a job well done," and devoting occasional or even frequent extra hours toward that job should be the criteria for promotion. Spending evenings and weekends demonstrating one's sociability and vying for executive attention should not.

Q. *Occasionally some of my company's clients call me "dear." Often the comment comes from older clients, and perhaps they don't realize they are offending anyone, so I am hesitant to say anything. How can I politely encourage these clients to call me by my given name?*

A. It is perfectly appropriate for you to say, "I prefer to be called Mary, please." Be sure, however, that you say it kindly and with the best of intentions since, as you note, the terms are usually not meant to be offensive.

Q. *Does the salutation for a business letter differ from that on a personal letter?*

A. No, there is no difference except that in a business letter the salutation is followed by a colon, while in a personal letter it is usually followed by a comma. What follows the word "dear" depends on your relationship with the recipient. If, when you speak to the vice president of marketing, you call him "Jim," you would begin your letter with "Dear Jim." If you call him "Mr. Wallace" in person, your letter would begin "Dear Mr. Wallace."

Q. *How does a married woman sign business correspondence?*

A. She signs her first name and the last name she uses for business. Women and men alike do not use a title in their signature.

Q. *What is the appropriate way to use business cards?*

A. Business cards are used in two main ways: When a business visit is made, a card is left as a record of the visit so that one's name, business firm, phone and fax numbers, and e-mail address are readily available. It is not necessary to leave a card on subsequent visits to the same firm. The other time business cards are used is when executives meet people with whom they want to establish or further a business contact. This could take place anywhere, from a convention to a cocktail party.

Q. *I can't tell you how many times I have picked up the phone to hear someone's secretary say: "Ms. Moore?*

Please hold for Mr. Jaffe." And I hold, and I hold, and I hold. These people are calling me. *Why should I have to waste my time waiting for them? Am I wrong?*

A. You are quite correct. It is inconsiderate for anyone to call you, engage your attention, and then keep you waiting. When a secretary places calls, his or her boss should be ready to pick up the phone as soon as contact is made.

Q. *May I invite my boss to lunch?*

A. In general, no. You may return an invitation to his or her home, because that becomes a social occasion. You don't, however, invite your boss to lunch during the normal course of business (although there are exceptions, such as when you've worked together for years).

Q. *When a group of business associates gathers for lunch, who pays?*

A. The one who issues the invitation is considered the host and is expected to pay for the lunch. If, on the other hand, a group of business associates plans to have lunch so they can spend an out-of-the-office hour together, each generally pays for his or her own lunch.

Q. *How does a businessman or -woman know if a social invitation includes spouses or partners?*

A. Usually the invitation is issued or addressed to both members of a couple. If, for some reason, you aren't sure if spouses are included, ask. If you are single, it's okay if you ask, "Should I bring a date (or friend) or would you rather I came alone?" If you are living with someone, your companion should be treated exactly as a spouse would be. If your partner has been excluded from the invitation because of your host's ignorance of the situation, all you need do is ask, "May I bring Susan Swanson, the woman I live with?" or "I live with Dave Ferris. Is it all right if I bring him?"

Q. *Who from my work world should I invite to my daughter's wedding?*

A. Your answer starts with the size of the guest list and your daughter's overall plans for the wedding. Be careful as well not to diminish your daughter's day by inviting a lot of people she does not know. If the wedding is small and personal, you should invite only those business people whom you consider personal friends—and their spouses. It's not a good idea to use a daughter's wedding to entertain clients, prospective clients, and business associates, but if you do, be careful not to slight anyone by failure to extend an invitation.

Q. *Who should I invite to my son's bar mitzvah?*

A. The answer depends on the size of the celebration of the occasion, as it does with a wedding. If the bar mitzvah is small and intimate, you need invite only friends, some of whom may be business associates. If it is large, you may want to invite everyone in your office. If the religious ceremony is not followed immediately by the party, you may even decide to omit business invitations to the religious service, extending them only to the party afterward.

Q. *What role does the spouse play in business entertaining?*

A. A spouse's role is to support you—to make your guests feel welcome, to help them enjoy being with you both, as well as to assist with refreshments. It is also your spouse's role to listen well, to ask questions and to show a tactful interest in your business and business associates. Your spouse should feel free to discuss his or her profession and personal concerns, too, so long as the topics are of general interest and he or she does not monopolize the conversation.

Q. *My husband and I are returning the dinner invitation of his employer by giving a small dinner party in our home. How does he extend the invitation?*

A. It's best if you extend the invitation—by mail or by phone—by contacting your husband's boss (and his or her spouse, if there is one) at his home. Your social invitation, outside of your husband's workplace, is preferable to his inviting his boss at work.

Q. *When giving a business dinner party at home without serving help, should both my husband and I greet guests at the door?*

A. Yes, whenever possible you both should be close by so that introductions can be made. One of you can then tend to other hosting duties while the other introduces guests to people they do not know.

Q. *A friend who has just become an insurance agent has asked to review our various policies to see if she can do better for us. I've always felt it is wiser not to mix friendship and business—what do you think?*

A. In general, I would agree with you. When one has a wide range of friends in a variety of service businesses, however, giving them your business is often an extension of that friendship. There are advantages to doing business with good friends; they are most likely people you trust who, to a greater extent than would another professional in the field, have your best interest in mind. If something goes wrong, however—if the new muffler on your car falls off; if your case in court is not successful; if your investment is slower to show growth than you had hoped—you and the friend have to separate business from friendship in analyzing the situation and not react personally. If you can keep the two separate, then a business involvement with a friend can be most satisfactory. As long as you don't expect special rates or favors, and as long as your friend is someone whose judgment and professionalism you respect, the relationship can be strengthened and mutually beneficial.

Q. *Several years ago my office was quite small and we celebrated one another's birthdays and other special occasions. Since then, the office has grown and the special occasions have gotten out of hand. It seems like almost every week someone is collecting for a birthday gift, funeral flowers, new baby gifts, or wedding gifts. It is getting too expensive, yet no one wants to hurt anyone's feelings by saying no. Have you any advice?*

A. Discuss the creation of a yearly department "kitty" where everyone chips in a set amount at the beginning of the year, to be allocated as need arises. Guidelines should be established at the same time. The group might decide, for example, to limit birthday acknowledgments to birthday cards and no gifts.

Q. *A car pool is required at my company, and it is a real nightmare because so many people aren't responsible about showing up on time or being ready when they are picked up. This may seem like a tactical problem, but I think it is an etiquette problem, too. It is simply rude to make others late to work. Do you agree?*

A. Yes, I do. This is an ongoing problem since many people these days do commute by car pool. If everyone in a car pool does not feel the same way about establishing and keeping schedules, it obviously is a problem. This is a time when being nice is not enough. You have the right to say, "Harry, you have to be ready on time from now on—you are making us all late at least three days a week." If the car pool is more than just you and Harry, you may even have to threaten: "Harry, if you can't be on time, you'll have to find another car pool. The rest of us can't afford to be late so regularly." This is not rude on your part.

Q. *I keep tissues, a radio, and some other personal items in my office. I often find that others have helped themselves to my tissues, taken my radio to listen to, or walked off with my stapler. Is there anything I can do to keep this kind of "borrowing" to a minimum?*

A. You should always keep anything you consider essential or invaluable in a safe place or locked in a desk drawer when you're away. Also, you can put up a little sign in your office requesting that coworkers ask your permission to borrow anything on your desk or leave a note when they do.

Q. *I work in an office cubicle, and a neighbor of mine has the terrible habit of using the speakerphone to check her messages and make calls. Is there anything I* *can say, or am I doomed to have to listen to her every message and call?*

A. Certainly, there is something you can say! Ask her if she minds either not retrieving her messages or speaking on her speakerphone—or at least turning the volume down. Tell her you're having difficulty concentrating over the noise and you'd appreciate her keeping it down.

Q. *Our office has a fairly conservative dress code, with men wearing suits and ties and women generally wearing suits or dresses. Now management is instigating Casual Fridays. What can we comfortably wear without looking too casual?*

A. While Casual Fridays vary from office to office, certain guidelines still apply. In general, Casual Fridays are defined as a dress-down version of the rest of the week's professional wear. The most important thing to remember is to maintain a neat, clean, professional appearance. Anything that looks sloppy, unclean, or in disrepair is generally off-limits. Suggestive or revealing clothing is a bad idea, as are sweatpants and sweatshirts. On a Casual Friday in a conservative office, the men might wear a crisp button-down or polo-style shirt with a sweater or vest and khaki pants, while women might wear a button-down or turtleneck shirt with khaki pants. Jeans may or may not be allowed. Some offices allow sneaker-type shoes; others prefer that employees stick with loafers or business shoes. There will likely be a guide or office policy that will spell out what's appropriate in your office. If not, ask your manager or human resources contact for some ideas.

Q. *Someone I work with has asked me to write a reference letter for him. The only problem is, I can think of little good to say about him. What do I do?*

A. Tell the truth; don't be derogatory but don't over-praise. Play up any positive points, and suggest that he has potential for growth. If you truly cannot think of one good thing to say about him, simply tell him you are not informed enough about his work to make an accurate assessment—and that you'll have to pass on writing the letter.

Q. *I am constantly being rattled by the sound of cellular phones and beepers going off in business meetings. Would I be out of line if I said something?*

A. Not at all: Smile, and in a nonthreatening way ask the person if he could please turn off his phone or beeper or at least turn down the volume. If you are in charge of a business meeting, you have every right to ask participants to turn off their machines in advance.

Q. *I was just downsized from my job. I was considered a model employee and always received stellar reviews* *from superiors, but the company's declining profits required a deep cutback in personnel. I'm embarrassed when people ask me about my job; do I have to say I was fired?*

A. Of course not. In these days of rampant downsizings, most people have the good sense to understand that many good workers are being let go, for no reason other than to help boost a company's bottom line. Simply say that you were downsized from a company looking for ways to cut costs.

Q. *We have a coworker who is always combing her hair, spraying her hair, and doing her nails at her desk. Can we say something to her to stop these offensive practices?*

A. It's best to have a boss or office manager talk to her in private. Grooming should be done in the privacy of office restrooms, never at the desk.

CHAPTER 6

KIDS AND TEENS

Q. *What names should children use when addressing their parents' friends?*

A. They should call them "Mr." or "Mrs." unless their parents' friends have requested that they call them by their first names or by nicknames.

Q. *My husband is named after his father and uses the suffix "Jr." after his name. We are naming our son after my husband's uncle. Do we attach a suffix after his name, and if so, would it also be "Jr."?*

A. Yes, he may receive a suffix after his name, but the suffix is "2nd." A child named after his grandfather (whose name is different from the child's father's), uncle, or cousin also is called "2nd," not "Jr." Were your son to be named after his father, who is named after his own father, the suffix would be "3rd."

Q. *Are there any guidelines for insisting on good manners from my children's friends? In our household, for example, we don't allow hats at the dinner table, and yet my daughter's boyfriend wears his baseball hat when he dines with us. My son's friend snaps and*

*cracks his gum when he is talking to us, which bothers
me. What may I say to them?*

A. You have to draw the line between the "When in
Rome" rules of etiquette and commentary on someone else's personal manners, or lack thereof. You have
every right to tell your daughter's boyfriend that
house rules include no hats at the dinner table. You
should say this to him in private, before he is seated at
the table. You do not have the right, however, to tell a
child who is not your own that it is rude to chew gum
loudly, that he should wear deodorant, or that he
should stand up when an adult enters the room—
unless he has asked you for advice. You can only hope
that the example set in your home inspires him to
acquire better personal manners.

Q. *What do I do when another child wants to play with
my daughter's toys? How do I explain the difference
between sharing and the right to her own possessions
when she shouldn't have to share, as with a stranger?*

A. Helping children learn to share their toys gives
them useful skills for later in life. There is a limit,
however. You can explain the difference to your
daughter by saying that children share with those who
are less fortunate, with friends and acquaintances, and
in group situations. She should always share when she
invites a friend to her house, and she would expect a
friend to share when invited to her house. She should

not expect to have to hand over her toys to someone she's just met, however, nor should she take someone's toys just because she wants them. The fact that a playground or beach is public does not mean that what we take to it becomes communal property.

Q. *A friend recently sent her child over to play with my daughter, and her child was obviously ill. This is not the first time this happened. How can I tactfully let parents know that I do not want their sick child visiting without sounding unkind or offensive?*

A. You could say that your child has been ill a lot lately, and you'd rather not expose her to too much sickness.

Q. *My thirteen-year-old daughter has a friend whose parents have very liberal ideas about raising kids. They are often absent on the weekends, leaving the kids on their own and unsupervised, and turning their home into a party hangout for junior-high students. I have limited my daughter's exposure to this friend and prohibited overnight visits, but this seems to have only made my daughter more determined to go there. Is there any way I can discuss the situation with her friend's parents?*

A. They probably won't change their viewpoint, but if you think it's worth a try, tactfully and politely request a meeting with the parents of your daughter's friends.

Express your concern about the lack of supervision. Offer to have their child stay at your house on weekends when they'll be away, or to chaperone any gathering. As for your daughter, know that she is at an impressionable age and is looking to define herself in a unique way, which may lead her at times to be at odds with your beliefs. Sit down with her and explain calmly but firmly the rules and guidelines you expect her to respect. She must understand that if she crosses the line, she should expect some punishment, such as being grounded. Ask her to invite her friend over more often, or offer to take them on some outings they would enjoy.

Q. *My husband and I have limited our children's TV-watching time. How can we enforce these rules when the kids sleep over at their friends' homes? Can we broach the subject with the friends' parents?*

A. Certainly you can, but that doesn't guarantee that they will follow your example. You can explain to them, however, which programs you deem off limits or unfit. It is inevitable that your child will be exposed to the world; you can't protect him forever. An evening of extra TV-watching every now and then should do little harm as long as your child is aware of the values that you deem important for your family.

Q. *My sixteen-year-old daughter has asked us to let her get birth-control pills. I appreciate her honesty, but* *think she is too young to be sexually active. I feel that procuring a prescription makes it appear as if I am giving a stamp of approval, yet I'd hate for her to have to go behind my back to do so. My daughter is a very responsible, emotionally mature teen who does well in school, and I think a pregnancy would be disastrous. What should I do?*

A. First, I would sit down with her and talk quite frankly about sex and its ramifications for someone of her age. You would be wise to discuss the importance of safeguarding against the AIDS virus and other sexually communicable diseases, which are not protected by birth control pills. Second, I agree that her honesty is preferable to going behind your back—she is showing respect and letting you know that your opinion is important to her. Third, the reality today is that more than half of teenagers in the country are sexually active. I say, if your daughter has a steady boyfriend, and both are responsible and mature, and you have counseled her on the ramifications of sexual behavior, you should consider acquiescing to her wishes.

Q. *Conspicuous consumption seems to start younger and younger these days. Children are under a lot of pressure to keep up with their peers in owning the latest toys and designer-label clothes. How can I give my kids some perspective on consumerism and how one's worth is not measured by the number toys you own?*

A. I have always believed in the value of "showing" children rather than lecturing to them. Here's a suggestion: Every Christmas, have your children rummage through their toys and pick out ones they are no longer interested in—and make sure the toys are in good shape. Then put them in a big box, from which you and your children distribute the toys to local hospitals, shelters, or charity organizations. You could also have your children use a small amount of their money saved each year to buy a new gift to put into the box. Including your child in volunteer work—distributing canned goods at Thanksgiving time or working in a soup kitchen—will also help plant the seeds of altruism. Your other way of obviously helping your children gain the outlook you strive for is to avoid buying them everything they say they "must have."

Q. *After teaching my child about "stranger danger," I find myself insisting that he be polite to and answer questions of people that I know, but who are strangers to him. This has to be confusing. Is there a way to explain the difference so that he is polite but careful?*

A. Explain that the strangers introduced to him by his family are not dangerous, because they are friends of yours. This puts these people in a different category than "stranger"; since they are friends of his mother and father, they become his friends, too.

Q. *My elderly mother is living at home with us. She is physically frail, but her mind is sharp. She is constantly yelling at my twelve-year-old son, however, who like most boys his age is high-spirited, loves rock music, and ball-playing. He is never rude to his grandmother, but she can be abusive to him. How can I get the message across to her that she needs to give him some breathing space—and let him be an adolescent boy?*

A. Simply by politely saying just that. And impress upon your son as well the importance of respecting his grandmother's space. Get her to talk about things that he may be fascinated with, like tales of his ancestors. If the situation worsens, however, you may want to consider an alternative living situation for your mother.

Q. *I am uncomfortable with the way a close friend disciplines her young child; I find it unnecessarily harsh. Would I be out of line if I said something to her about it?*

A. If your friend is indeed a close one, you may ask her whether she is getting results from her style of discipline. Or you might give her, in a nonjudgmental, simply-for-her-own-information manner, any articles, books, or videotapes that recommend less harsh methods of discipline. If your friend is not a close one, you're better off keeping your feelings to yourself—unless, of course, you sense that the discipline has crossed over into abuse.

CHAPTER 7

GUESTS AND HOSTS

Q. *What do you consider the hallmarks of a good guest? of a good host and hostess?*

A. A good guest is enthusiastic, congenial, and considerate, treating other guests, the host and hostess, and the host and hostess' property with thoughtfulness and respect. A good host and hostess are well prepared to see to the needs of each of their guests, having carefully planned for their comfort and entertainment.

Q. *When visiting the home of friends who own pets, is it proper for me to protest their dog's jumping on me without appearing rude?*

A. Yes. Remain pleasant and simply ask that the animal be put in another room. Say, "I'm sorry, but cats (or dogs) really bother me—" or, "My allergies have gotten so much worse—would you mind removing Tabby (or Fido) from the room until I leave?" A good host will automatically keep animals away when visitors are new acquaintances.

Q. *My dog is very well behaved. Is there any reason why I can't take her with me when I visit friends?*

A. The best reason is that if the dog is not invited, it belongs at home. Even if the person you are visiting loves animals, you should never just show up with a pet or ask whether you may bring a pet along on a visit. Doing so only puts your host and hostess in a difficult position. Naturally, your pet may go if your host suggests it on his own. Be sure, before you accept on its behalf, that your pet's behavior will be exemplary. You should never, ever take a dog to anyone's house that is not perfectly house-trained, chews things, or will not stay off furniture.

Q. *What can I do if children of friends are brought along on an adults-only visit?*

A. If you wish to be gracious, you must invite them in. If the children are small, however, and you have valuable objects that could be damaged, you may ask them to wait a moment while you remove the objects from harm's way, mentioning that you weren't expecting the children. Put paper and markers or crayons on the kitchen table, offer a snack, or find a suitable program on television to keep the children occupied while you and your friends talk. Other than providing these diversions, you are not obligated in any way to entertain the children; it is the parents' responsibility alone to make sure they are well behaved and occupied.

Q. *Several of my friends have young children. I do not.*

What preparations can you suggest making before they visit?

A. Remove from low tables breakable articles and things that might be dangerous to a small child. Shut the doors to rooms you wish to be off limits and make sure the doors to cellar steps and low windows are tightly closed or locked. Put together a basket of simple toys–coloring books, crayons, even plastic and wooden cooking utensils and pots and pans. These go a long way toward making the visit enjoyable for both parent and host. If you have absolutely nothing on hand to entertain a child, ask the parents to bring a bag of toys or a video along so the children can be kept busy and happy during the visit. It's also a good idea to have a supply of cookies or crackers and milk or juice available to fill in when the novelty of playing in a different environment wears off.

Q. *The law has pretty much eliminated any questions about smoking in public places, but is it all right to smoke in a friend's home?*

A. It is safe to assume that you are not to smoke in anyone's home unless they do themselves. Today, with unanswered questions about the dangers of second-hand smoke, even those hosts who previously didn't mind may mind now. If you must have a cigarette, ask your host if you may step outside for a few minutes for one. Even when your host smokes cigarettes, you should not light a pipe or cigar indoors unless you request permission first. Never smoke around infants or small children. In a club where smoking is allowed, it still is courteous to ask those with you if they mind if you smoke. Lastly, remember not to walk around or dance with a cigarette in your hand or mouth.

Q. *Am I obligated to entertain an unexpected guest?*

A. Not at all. If you have prior plans, those plans take precedence over entertaining an unexpected guest. If someone arrives unexpectedly from a long distance and you are planning to leave for a large or informal party or gathering, check with your host to see if you can bring your guest along. If, however, you are expected at a small dinner party or for bridge, ask your guest to make herself at home until you return. If possible, find something in the refrigerator that will serve as a snack or light meal.

When the visitor is from nearby, you merely apologize and say you were just leaving for an engagement. Ask whether the visitor can return another time, and make the future date right then. A firm invitation proves that you would really enjoy a visit at a more convenient time. If your earlier plans were such that they could be carried out on another day, the polite thing to do is postpone them and stay at home with your visitor.

If an unexpected guest arrives as you are about to sit down to dinner, the polite thing to do is to make the meal stretch to include them. If they decline, pull up a chair for them, offer them a cup of coffee or a cold drink, and ask their forgiveness while you finish your meal.

Q. *I would like to know what I should do with bedding the morning after I've stayed overnight at a friend's.*

A. Remove the sheets and pull up the bedspread neatly. Fold the sheets and leave them at the foot of the bed or take them to the laundry room. Your hostess can then make up the bed at her leisure.

Q. *I always ask my company to take off their shoes because I don't want my new rugs and carpets soiled. Some oblige graciously; some oblige but get offended. What do you suggest?*

A. If you can lay a piece of indoor-outdoor carpeting leading to your entry and a good doormat at the door, your carpets should not get soiled. If you still feel you must ask people to remove their shoes, buy a supply of slippers such as those the airlines give out on long trips and put them by the door for guests to use.

Q. *The invitation says dinner at 7:30. What time should I arrive at the party?*

A. The answer depends on the custom in your area. If the custom is that guests are not expected to arrive until fifteen minutes to half an hour after the stated hour, it is wise to follow this practice. Otherwise you should arrive no later than fifteen minutes after the hour given and never earlier.

Q. *Is the guest of honor at a party supposed to be the first guest to leave or the last?*

A. The guest of honor is traditionally the first to leave. This rule is obsolete, however—today the guest of honor is free to stay as long as he likes. The only time the rule is followed is when the guest of honor is the president of the United States or another dignitary, in which case no one may leave before he or she does.

Q. *How long should a hostess delay dinner for a late-arriving guest?*

A. Fifteen minutes is the established length of time. To wait more than twenty minutes, at the outside, would be showing rudeness to many for the sake of one. When the late guest finally arrives, he or she should apologize to the hostess and be seated.

Q. *When a guest arrives late and we've already finished the first course, is that course served to the late-arriving guest?*

A. No, the latecomer is served whatever course is being eaten at the time he or she arrives, unless the course is dessert, in which case he or she would be served the entrée while others have their dessert.

Q. *How long should a guest remain at a party? How does one know when to call it a night?*

A. Try to be sensitive and aware of the people around you. Most hostesses are reluctant to try to "speed the parting guest," so make an effort to observe when your hosts and other party guests begin to look tired. You should stay for at least one hour after dinner—it is hardly complimentary to the hostess to "eat and run." At a small party, don't leave long before anyone else seems ready to go—your departure may break up the party.

If you are taking your leave from a large party, locate your host and hostess and thank them for a lovely evening. Insist that there is no need for them to see you to the door, find your belongings, and let yourself out.

At a small gathering, say your good-byes to the other guests, thank your host and hostess, find your coat, and leave.

•

Q. *How can I discourage my guests from mixing their own drinks in my home?*

A. It is difficult to do without being insulting. You can control the situation somewhat, however, by going to the bar with your guest and asking them to get out the ice or the mix or whatever while you pour the liquor yourself. You can also avoid having more than one bottle of liquor in evidence if guests seem to be heavy drinkers. Make it obvious that you use a jigger to pour drinks and hand the shot glass to your guests before they pour themselves one.

Q. *How do I handle an inebriated guest?*

A. You first refuse to serve him or her more liquor. While this may make him become abusive, that is preferable to having him become more intoxicated. You are then responsible for seeing that the drunken guest is taken home. You may ask a friend to drive him, you can go yourself if the distance isn't great, or you can call a cab, give the directions, and pay for it. The person's car keys should be taken away from him if he is not willing to go home with someone else. If your guest has reached the point of almost passing out, put him in a bed to sleep it off overnight. If the inebriated person has a spouse or date present, you should offer this person accommodations, too, or see that he or she gets home safely.

Q. *I got drunk at a party. Should I have called my hosts the next day and apologized?*

A. Yes, if your behavior was insulting or rude and if you disrupted the party. If you felt yourself getting drunk, however, and left the party without embarrassing yourself, the other guests, or your hosts, there is really little to apologize for except perhaps an early departure. You can mention this when you make your thank-you call by saying, "I'm sorry to have left a little early, but I wasn't feeling well and thought it best to go."

Q. *May I offer to help my hostess serve or clear the table?*

A. Yes, you may offer, but don't insist if she refuses your help. Most hostesses want you to relax, or prefer to follow their own system of organization by themselves.

Q. *I am the mother of a preschooler and an infant. My husband and I have several friends who come to visit and stay past 2 A.M.! Is it ever acceptable to ask them to leave? If so, how do we broach the subject?*

A. You may certainly suggest that they leave by saying, "Well, this has been great fun, but the baby will have us up by six or earlier, and we've really got to get to bed." When guests outstay their welcome at a home where there are no children, it is also effective to say, with good humor, "Well, Pat, we'd better go to bed; these poor folks must want to go home!"

Q. *My husband and I are members of the geriatric set and are in a dilemma over potential houseguests. Our*

*dear friends from 300 miles away have asked if they
could come visit us for an extended period of time. The
problem is that they have two youngsters, ages three
and five, who are undisciplined and quite a handful, as
we discovered when they came to visit last year. My
wife and I simply cannot handle these kids in close
quarters again. How do we say so to our friends without
hurting their feelings?*

A. Very nicely and diplomatically express your situation to them in a letter or over the phone. Tell them that at your age, you simply do not have the energy to have the four of them stay in your home. While making it clear that their visit means a great deal to you, ask whether they wouldn't mind either staying for only one or two nights in your home or staying in a motel nearby. You can even offer suggestions on motels and hotels in the area. And, if your finances are sufficient and you don't think it would insult them, you can even offer to pay for half or all of their motel stay.

Q. *My second wife and I host an annual Christmas
party for our friends (no children invited). I have
always included my ex-wife, because we have remained
on friendly terms and we share mutual friends. This
year, however, after six years of marriage, my wife has
decided that she would prefer that my ex-wife not
attend. What do I do?*

A. After six years of marriage—and I assume you are happily married—you should acquiesce to your wife's wishes. Explain to your ex-wife as kindly as possible that your new wife is simply not comfortable with her being there.

Q. *I am always faced with this dilemma—whether to invite two people to the same party who were once serious lovers but are no longer involved. What do I do?*

A. A serious love affair is vastly different from a fling, especially when the break-up was a traumatic one. Either way, you should never do anything to make a guest feel uncomfortable. So, if doing so makes either person unhappy (you can ask either or both of them), don't invite both to the same party.

CHAPTER 8

MEALTIME MANNERS

Q. *I find myself somewhat intimidated when I'm dining as a guest in someone's home or at a formal occasion. Can you give me some basic guidelines on mealtime manners?*

A. Consideration for others is the rule governing good table manners. Whether you're seated across the dinner table from a U.S. senator or your host's fifteen-year-old son, show that person respect by demonstrating good table manners. Here are answers to some of the most common questions regarding manners at the dinner table.

Q. *What is the correct way to use a knife and fork?*

A. The American custom of "zigzag" eating (changing the fork from the left to the right hand after cutting) is perfectly correct. The knife is put down on the plate after cutting and the fork is raised to the mouth, tines up. Equally correct is the European method of leaving the fork in the left hand after cutting and raising it to the mouth in the same position in which it was held for cutting, tines down. The knife may also be used as a "pusher" if necessary. To do so, hold the knife in the left hand in the same position as when cutting with the right hand, and the tip of the blade helps to guide and push the food onto the fork.

Q. *What is the correct placement for silverware?*

A. When the main course is finished, the knife and fork are placed beside each other on the dinner plate diagonally from upper left to lower right, the handles extended slightly over the edge of the plate. The dessert spoon and/or fork is placed in the same position on the plate when the diner has finished. If dessert is served in a stemmed or deep bowl on another plate, the dessert spoon is put down on the plate, never left in the bowl.

Q. *What is the rule regarding elbows on the table?*

A. In some situations elbows are not only permitted on the table but actually necessary. This is true in noisy restaurants or clubs, where the only way to hear above the music and chatter is to lean far forward. One is far more graceful leaning forward supported by his or her elbows than doubled forward over hands in the lap. At a formal dinner, elbows may be on the table because again one has to lean forward in order to talk to a companion at a distance across the table. Even in these special situations, elbows are never on the table when one is eating.

Q. *When there are several forks and spoons laid out in a place setting, how do I know which to use—and when?*

A. You always start with the implement of each type that is farthest from the plate. Of course, if the table is incorrectly set, and you realize that you cannot use the implement for the course that its position indicates, you should, of course, choose the next one that is appropriate. Otherwise, start at the outside, working your way with each course toward the center.

Q. *What is the correct way to hold flatware?*

A. Lightly. The fork and spoon are held with the thumb and forefinger at a position on the fork that is comfortable, usually about three-quarters of the way up the handle. Your other three fingers then fit loosely and comfortably behind the handle, with the middle finger serving as a support from underneath.

Q. *When is reaching across the dinner table allowed?*

A. Stretching, to retrieve a serving dish, say, is only correct when it does not involve stretching across your neighbor or leaning far across the table yourself. If the item you want is not close at hand, simply ask the person closest to it to pass it to you.

Q. *When I pass the salt, should I also pass the pepper?*

A. There is no rule that says you have to pass both at once.

Q. *How does one hold a serving spoon and fork?*

A. When lifting food from a serving dish, the spoon is held underneath, with the fork prongs turned down to help hold the portion on the spoon.

Q. *When is it proper to ask for second helpings?*

A. The circumstances determine whether or not it is acceptable to ask for seconds at a dinner party. It is not acceptable at a formal dinner but is permissible at an informal one. At a formal dinner, second helpings are to be offered.

Q. *How does one break bread at the dinner table?*

A. Help yourself to bread using your fingers. Place the bread, roll, crackers, or whatever on your butter plate. Don't butter the whole piece at once, but instead break off manageable pieces, and butter and eat them one at a time.

WHEN I'M A GUEST AT A DINNER PARTY, WHAT DO I DO WHEN I . . .

Q. . . . *need to cough, sneeze, or blow my nose?*

A. You should excuse yourself from the table and go to the restroom to blow your nose. You might find it necessary to first blow your nose (by way of a few gentle puffs) using your handkerchief or tissue immediately following a sneeze. Do not use your napkin to blow your nose. Before returning to the table, be sure to wash your hands thoroughly after you're through.

Q. . . . *discover bugs, hair, or other nonedibles in the food?*

A. Try to remove the object without calling attention to it and continue eating. If you are truly repulsed, leave the dish untouched rather than embarrass your hostess in a private home. At a restaurant you may—and should—quietly point out the critter to your waiter and ask for a replacement dish. If the alien object has reached your mouth without your previously noticing it, remove it with your fingers as inconspicuously as possible and place it at the edge of your plate.

Q. . . . *get food stuck in a tooth?*

A. It is not permissible to use a toothpick or to use your fingers to pick at your teeth when at the table. If something stuck in your tooth is actually hurting, excuse yourself from the table and go to the bathroom to remove it. Otherwise, wait until the end of the meal and then go take care of it, asking for a toothpick if necessary.

Q. . . . *spill something?*

A. Pick up jelly, a bit of vegetable, or other solid food with the blade of your knife or a clean spoon. If the spill has caused a stain, and you are at someone's house, dab a little water from your glass on it with the corner of your napkin. Apologize to your hostess, who, in turn, should not add to your embarrassment by calling attention to the accident. At an informal dinner without help, offer to get a cloth or sponge to mop up the liquid and help the hostess clean up in any way you can.

Q. . . . *begin choking on meat or bones?*

A. If a sip of water does not help but a good cough will, cover your mouth with your napkin and cough. Remove the morsel with your fingers and put it on the edge of your plate. If you continue to cough, excuse yourself from the table. In the event that you are really choking, you will be unable to speak. Don't hesitate to get someone's attention to help you. The seriousness of your condition will quickly be recognized, and it is no time to worry about manners. Keeping calm and acting quickly might well save your life.

Q. *. . . am faced with a finger bowl?*

A. Finger bowls are generally small glass bowls filled halfway to three-quarters of the way with cold water and are most often seen at formal meals. They are there for the purpose of freshening one's fingers after a meal, or after eating a hands-on food such as snails, corn on the cob, or hard-shelled seafood. Finger bowls are placed at the side of each diner's place after a hands-on dinner, or on the dessert plate at a formal dinner.

Dip your fingers, one hand at a time, into the water and then dry your fingers on your napkin. If a finger bowl is brought directly before dessert, it is often placed on a doily on the dessert plate. To remove it, lift it, with the doily underneath, and move it to the upper left of your place setting.

A slice of lemon is never used in a finger bowl at a formal dinner, but flowers may be floated in it. Lemon may be floated in a finger bowl used after a lobster dinner.

In some restaurants, moist steamed hand towels are brought to the table at the conclusion of the meal. These are held in tongs and presented to the diner. Take the towel, use it to wipe your hands and, if necessary, around your mouth. Diligent waiters will hover and take the towel from you the minute you are finished. If your waiter disappears, just put the towel at the side of your place on the table.

Q. *. . . have to use a saltcellar?*

A. Some hostesses prefer to use old-fashioned saltcellars, which salt shakers have largely replaced. If there is no spoon in the saltcellar, use the tip of a clean knife to take some salt. If the saltcellar is for you alone, you may either use the tip of your knife or you may take a pinch with your fingers. If it is to be shared with others, never use your fingers or a knife that is not clean. Salt that is to be dipped into should be put on the bread-and-butter plate or on the rim of whatever plate is before you.

Q. *. . . eat food that is too hot or food that tastes spoiled?*

A. If a bite of food is too hot, quickly take a swallow of water. If there is no cold beverage at all, and your mouth is scalding, you can spit the food out, preferably onto your fork or into your fingers, and from there place it quickly on the edge of the plate. The same is true of spoiled food. Should you eat a bad oyster or clam, for example, don't swallow it. Remove it as quickly and unobtrusively as you can. To spit anything whatsoever into the corner of your napkin is not permissible.

Q. *Can you suggest any dos and don'ts for dining?*

A. Consideration for others is the rule governing good table manners. You should not let anyone see what you have in your mouth or make noises while eating.

Avoid making a mess of the food on your plate. When cutting meat, keep your elbows at your side, or you risk poking your neighbor. Try not to scrape or drag chairs, rattle knives and forks against the plate, or make other unnecessary noises that can annoy those seated nearby. Do attempt to make pleasant conversation with your dining companions. In addition, there are other "don'ts" everyone should try and avoid:

- Don't talk with food in your mouth.
- Don't wave your silverware around when talking. Put it down on your plate.
- Don't encircle your plate with your arm.
- Don't push your plate back when finished.
- Don't lean back and announce "I'm through" or "I'm stuffed." Putting your utensils down across your plate shows that you have finished.
- Don't put liquid in your mouth if it is already filled with food.
- Don't crook your finger when picking up a cup or glass. It's an affected mannerism.
- Don't ever leave your spoon in your cup, soup bowl, or in a stemmed glass.
- Don't cut up your entire meal before you start to eat. Cut only one or two bites at a time.
- Don't take huge mouthfuls of anything.
- Don't leave half the food on your spoon or fork. Learn to put less on and then eat it in one bite.
- Don't wear an excessive amount of lipstick to the table. Not only can it stain napkins, but it also looks unattractive on the rims of cups and glasses

or on the silver.
- Don't wipe off the tableware in a restaurant. If your silverware is dirty, ask the waiter or waitress for a clean set.

Q. *Does the table setting for a family dinner differ from the table setting when guests join the family for dinner?*

A. The main difference between a table setting for guests and a table setting for family is that for the latter a minimum of utensils and plates is put at each place setting. Butter plates and knives are often omitted for family dinners, and the bread and butter are placed at the edge of the dinner plate, for example. What is important is that good manners are practiced, as well as graciousness and consideration for others—be they family or guests.

HOW IS THE TABLE SET FOR . . .

Q. . . . *a formal meal?*

A. There is only one rule for a formal table, and that is that everything must be geometrically spaced—the centerpiece in the actual center, the places at equal distances, and all utensils balanced.

A formal place setting consists of:

- **Service plate**, positioned so the pattern "picture" faces the diner.
- **Butter plate**, placed above the forks at the left of the place setting.
- **Glasses**, positioned according to size.
- **Salad fork**, placed directly to the left of the plate, assuming salad is served with or after the entrée (if salad is served as a first course, the salad fork is placed to the left of the dinner fork).

- **Meat fork**, positioned to the left of the salad fork.
- **Fish fork**, positioned to the left of the meat fork. Since it is used first, it is farthest from the plate.
- **Salad knife**, just to the right of the plate (as noted above, the knife would go to the right of the dinner knife if salad is served first).
- **Meat knife**, placed to the right of the salad knife.
- **Fish knife**, positioned to the right of the meat knife.
- **Butter knife**, positioned diagonally at the top of the butter plate.
- **Soup spoon and/or fruit spoon** placed outside the knives.
- **Oyster fork**, if shellfish is to be served, beyond the spoons. This is the only fork ever placed on the right.
- **Napkin**.

No more than three of any one implement are ever placed on the table (with the exception of an oyster fork, making four forks). If more than three courses are served before dessert, therefore, the fork for the fourth course is brought in with the course; or the salad fork and knife may be omitted in the beginning and brought in when salad is served.

Dessert spoons and forks are brought in on the dessert plate just before dessert is served.

Q. . . . *a less formal meal?*

A. As at a formal dinner, everything on the table should be symmetrically and evenly spaced. Otherwise, you have much more latitude in planning an informal, casual, or semiformal dinner than you do for a formal dinner. You may use color in your table linens or other table appointments. Candles are used, just as they are on formal dinner tables, but usually as single candles rather than candelabra. They may be of any color that complements your table setting, but they must be high or low enough so that the flame is not at the eye level of the diners.

For an informal place setting, there is less of everything. There are fewer courses served, so fewer pieces of silverware are set out. The typical place setting for an informal, three-course dinner includes:

- **Two forks**, one for dinner placed at the far left and one for dessert or salad positioned directly to the left of the plate.
- **Dinner plate**, which is not on the table when guests sit down.

- **Salad plate**, to the left of the forks.
- **Butter plate**, placed above the forks.
- **Dinner knife**, next to the plate on the right (for steak, chops, chicken, or game birds it may be a steak knife).
- **Butter knife**, placed diagonally across the butter plate.
- **Two spoons**, a dessert spoon positioned to the right of the knife, and if soup is to be served, a soup spoon to the right of the dessert spoon.
- **Water goblet**, placed above the knife.
- **Wineglass**, positioned slightly forward and to the right of the water goblet.
- **Napkin**, may be placed either in the center of the place setting or, if there is no salad plate, to the left of the forks.

Service plates are not used at an informal dinner, except in an appropriate size and style under a stemmed glass used for shrimp cocktail, fruit cup, etc., and under soup plates.

The dinner plate should not be on the table when you sit down, assuming you wish it to be warm when the food is served.

If you plan to serve coffee with the meal, the cup and saucer go to the right of the setting, with the coffee spoon on the table at the right of or placed on the saucer, bowlside up.

Q. . . . *a family-style meal?*

A. Practicality is the keynote in setting the table for family meals. A minimum number of utensils is put at each place—only those that are absolutely necessary. Since there is usually only one course and dessert, there may be only three pieces of silver—a fork, a knife, and a spoon for the dessert. If you are having soup or fruit first, utensils for those foods must be added. It is not necessary to have separate salad forks, although individual salad bowls should be set out.

Frozen dinners should not be eaten from the containers, but should be spooned out onto warm plates.

Ketchup, jellies, pickles, and other condiments may be served from their jars if no guests are present. The jars should be on saucers, and each should have its own separate serving spoon or fork on the saucer. Paper napkins are perfectly correct for family meals. Since no china or silverware that will not be used need be placed on the table, the following setting may be used, according to your menu:

- **Dinner fork** at the left of the plate.
- **Dinner knife** at the right of the plate, then the soup spoon, the shellfish fork, or the dessert spoon on the outside.
- **Glass or goblet** for a beverage at the right above the knife.
- **Butter plate**, if used, to the left and above the fork, with the butter knife laid on it diagonally from the upper left to the lower right.
- **Salad plate** at the left of the fork.
- **Napkin** at the left or in the center of the setting.
- **Coffee mug** or cup and saucer with a spoon at the right.

If the food is to be passed, dinner plates should already be in place on the table when the family sits down or stacked in front of the head of the household if he or she is to serve. Often plates are served directly from the stove in order to avoid the use of extra platters and serving dishes.

Q. *What should a guest do when dining with a family of another faith who say grace before meals: sit quietly or join in?*

A. A guest certainly may join in if he or she feels comfortable doing so. If your hosts ask you to join hands during the prayer, this is simply a gesture of loving friendship and in no way means you are practicing their faith by doing so. However, it is not necessary for guests to cross themselves, even though their Catholic hosts do so—nor is it necessary to make any gesture not practiced in their own faith. If a guest chooses not to join in grace, he or she may sit (or stand) quietly until grace is finished. A clue as to whether grace is to be said is whether the hostess immediately puts her napkin in her lap. If she does not, it is a signal that she may be waiting to say grace as soon as everyone is silent. Some faiths say grace after the meal is concluded—look to your hostess for a signal if one should rise from table after the meal is finished, or wait for a prayer to be said.

Q. *What is the proper way to handle a napkin at dinner?*

A. Ordinarily, as soon as you are seated, you may put your napkin in your lap. At a formal dinner, however, you wait for your hostess to put hers on her lap first. Remove the napkin from the table, place it on your lap, and unfold it as much as necessary. Never tuck it in to your collar, belt, or between buttons of a shirt. When using your napkin, blot or pat your lips—never wipe with it as if it were a washcloth. At the end of the meal, or anytime you leave the table during the meal, put the napkin on the left side of your place; if the plates have been removed, leave your napkin in the center. It should not be crumpled up, nor should it be refolded; rather, it is laid on the table in loose folds so that it does not spread itself out. At a formal dinner party, the hostess lays her napkin on the table as a signal that the meal is over, and the guests then lay their napkins on the table—not before.

Q. *When I'm a guest at a dinner party, how do I know when to start eating?*

A. It is the hostess' responsibility to ask guests to start on a hot course after three or four people have been served. Although most of us have been raised to wait for the hostess to "lift her fork" before starting, this is true only for a first course and for dessert. If the hostess forgets to encourage guests to begin, it is not incorrect for them to start eating a hot entrée once three or four people have been served.

Q. *Which glasses are used for which wines? Where are the glasses placed?*

A. Red wine, which is served at room temperature, is poured into round-bowled, stemmed glasses.

Red wine glass

White wine, which is served chilled, is poured into less rounded, more tulip-shaped glasses that are narrower at the rim than are red wine glasses.

White wine glass

Champagne, which is served well chilled, is poured into either flat, wide-rimmed glasses or into champagne flutes—which are long, narrow-stemmed glasses.

Sherry, which is served at room temperature, is poured into small, V-shaped glasses.

Flute

Sherry Glass

Wine glasses are placed on the table according to size so that the smaller ones are not hidden behind the larger ones. The water goblet is placed directly above the knives at the right of the plates. The champagne glass or flute is next to it at a slight distance to the right. The claret or red wine glass, or the white wine glass, is positioned in front of and between the water goblet and champagne glass. The sherry glass is placed either to the right or in front of the wineglass. Rather than grouping the wineglasses, you may place them in a straight row slanting downward from the water goblet at the upper left to the sherry glass at the lower right.

Q. *May a dinner guest ask the hostess for an item that does not appear on the table, such as mustard when ham is served?*

A. If an accompaniment that is ordinarily served is missing, it is obviously an oversight, and it is perfectly proper to ask for it. You should not, however, ask for anything unusual that your hostess might not have.

Q. *May I refuse a dish at dinner I dislike?*

A. If you are among friends, you may refuse with a polite "No, thank you." Otherwise it is good manners to take at least a little of every dish that is offered to you and put it onto your plate. You need not give your reason for refusing a dish, but if it is because of an allergy, diet, or other physical cause, you may quietly explain to your hostess without drawing the attention of the entire table. When declining a dish offered by a waiter, say "No, thank you," quietly. At a buffet dinner you need only help yourself to those dishes that appeal to you.

Q. *I attended a lunch the other day and was served beautiful open-faced sandwiches on English muffins. I was at a loss, however, on the best way to eat them. Should I have cut up the sandwich and eaten the bites with a fork, or could I have picked it up with my fingers and taken a bite?*

A. It depends on several factors. One, if the open-faced sandwich is small and fairly self-contained, so that it doesn't fall to pieces when you pick it up with fingers, you may do so. Second, if the sandwich is large and unwieldy or slathered in gravy or sauce, common sense tells you to cut it up and eat it with a fork. And third, the way you eat an open-faced sandwich depends on the occasion. If you are attending a formal dinner, you should eat the sandwich with a knife and fork.

Q. *In whose name are restaurant reservations made?*

A. Reservations are usually made in one name only. They are made in the name of the host or hostess who is giving the dinner party or, if a group of friends plan to meet at a restaurant and each will pay for his own meal, the reservation may be made in the name of the person who is delegated to make it, or in the name of anyone else in the group.

Q. *Who leads the way to the table, the man or the woman?*

A. Women generally walk behind the headwaiter or restaurant host, and the men follow them. But if a man is giving a dinner for six or more, the women would have to wait at the table until told by their host where to sit. In this case it causes less confusion if he goes in ahead of his guests. When a couple are hosts, the woman seats the guests, usually going first with the most important lady, and the host follows last.

Q. *When a man and woman are dining at a restaurant with a view, who gets the better seat?*

A. In a social situation, the woman is given the better seat, unless for some reason she prefers another seat. In this case she stands beside the other chair, saying, "I'd rather sit here if I may." If the meal is a business one, the client or more senior individual gets the better seat—regardless of whether or not that person is male or female.

Q. *If several people are meeting at a restaurant, does the first arriving diner take a table, or should he wait for the others?*

A. The first arrival should wait for the second rather than go in and sit alone, unless the first arrival sees that the restaurant is filling up and there may shortly be no tables left. When two arrive together, they should ask to be seated, explaining to the headwaiter that others are joining them and asking him to see that they are directed to the table. This avoids overcrowding the entry and sometimes is the only way of holding a reservation. Some restaurants, however, will not seat a group until all members are present.

Q. *Who gives the order to the waiter? I thought the woman was supposed to tell her choice to the gentleman with whom she was dining, and he conveyed it to the waiter. Is this still done?*

A. For many years, a woman dining with a man never spoke to the waiter herself. Today it is perfectly correct for a woman to give her order directly to the waiter. Many waiters ask the woman for her order first in an effort to be polite, and there is no reason why she should not answer directly.

Q. *On a restaurant menu what do* table d'hôte *and* à la carte *mean?*

A. *Table d'hôte* means a set price for a complete meal, irrespective of how many courses are offered. "Club" breakfasts and lunches, "blue plate" dinners, or any meals at fixed prices are table d'hôte. Usually, choices of an appetizer or soup, an entrée with vegetables, salad, dessert, and coffee are included in the one price.

Another type of table d'hôte menu is one that has a price beside each entrée. This price varies, but includes the full range of courses at that price. Sometimes a table d'hôte menu will show a price after a particular item, noting, for example, "shrimp cocktail, $3.00 extra." This means the full meal is included in the fixed price, plus the additional amount if shrimp cocktail is ordered instead of an appetizer that does not have its own price.

À la carte means that you may order from a list of dishes and pay the price listed beside each dish—even for your vegetable, salad, and coffee. Very often a separate card or a box insert on the à la carte menu offers a special dinner at one price, but if you order any item from the regular bill of fare, it will be charged as an extra.

Q. *How do restaurant table manners differ from the manners one uses at home?*

A. Although table manners are much the same whether

you are eating at home or at a restaurant, a few special situations arise when dining out.

- When vegetables and potatoes are served in individual side dishes, you may eat them directly from small dishes or put them on your dinner plate by using a serving spoon or sliding them directly out of the small dish. Ask the waiter to remove any empty dishes, to avoid an overcrowded table.

- When an uncut loaf of bread is placed on the table, the host—or the diner closest to the bread—slices or breaks off two or three individual portions and offers them with the rest of the loaf in the breadbasket or on the plate to the people beside him. This is then passed around the table for diners to cut the bread for themselves and possibly their neighbors.

- If coffee or tea is placed on the table without first having been poured by the waiter, the person nearest the pot should offer to pour, filling his or her own cup last.

- If sugar, crackers, cream, or other accompaniments to meals are served with paper wrappers or in plastic or cardboard containers, the wrappers should be crumpled up tightly and either tucked under the rim of your plate or placed on the edge of the saucer or butter plate. Don't put them in the ashtray if smokers are present, since their lighted cigarettes could easily set the paper on fire.

- Don't wipe off tableware in a restaurant. If your

silverware is dirty, simply ask the waiter or waitress for a clean replacement. If you spill wine or water in a restaurant, try quietly to attract the attention of the waiter to have it cleaned up.

- When you are dining at a restaurant buffet, never go back to the buffet for a refill with a dirty plate. Leave it for the waitperson to pick up and start afresh with a clean plate. When you are a guest at a buffet in someone's home, it is fine to use your soiled plate if seconds are offered.

- Tasting another person's food at the table is permissible if done unobtrusively. Never reach over and spear something off someone else's plate, however, or feed someone across the table. Either hand your fork to your dinner partner, have them spear a bite and then hand it back to you, or have them place a portion on your plate.

- At the end of a meal, a woman may quickly put on a little lipstick, but to look in a mirror and daub at the face is in bad taste.

- The one never-to-be-broken rule is: Never use a comb at a restaurant table—or in any public place. Never rearrange or put your hands to your hair in any place where food is served. These rules apply to both men and women.

Q. *I'd like to be able to take our children along with us when we dine out. What are some basic guidelines I can tell them in preparation?*

A. Good table manners begin at home, and children are never too young to learn to be well-behaved in the company of others. It's smart to start early, because bad habits are hard to break at an older age. Use the following guidelines to teach your children the rudiments of good table manners.

BE NEAT AND CLEAN. Make hand-washing a habit. Teach your child to wash his hands and face before he comes to a table to eat. Instead of ordering children to do this, tell them why. Explain about germs and how pleasant it is to eat and talk with someone who made herself look nice, out of respect for everyone else. When children understand the reason for doing something, it is easier for them to remember to do it.

EAT IN SMALL BITES. First, because it isn't safe to have more in your mouth than you can manage, and second, because it is unattractive to sit with anyone who can't close his lips or who has bits of food spewing from his mouth. Thus, chew with the mouth closed.

DO NOT FLOAT FOOD DOWN YOUR THROAT WITH DRINKS. Again, there is a safety factor at work, but there is also a politeness factor, since a child has to open a mouthful of food in order to swallow a beverage. A rule could be that the mouth opens to receive a spoonful or forkful of food, and it doesn't open again until that food is chewed, with the mouth closed, and swallowed.

FOOD NOISES ARE UNACCEPTABLE. Lips are not smacked; drinks are not gulped.

NAPKINS, NOT SLEEVES OR HANDS, ARE FOR WIPING MOUTHS. They are meant to be used regularly throughout the meal. Why? Because it is hard for anyone to know if he has a milk mustache or ketchup on his cheek unless others point it out to him. Using the napkin periodically takes care of what otherwise might be an embarrassing sight.

THERE IS A CORRECT WAY TO HOLD AND USE UTENSILS. Start out with younger children using a spoon. By five or six years of age, most children can learn to be adept at using a fork and knife. By age six, children should learn how to cut food and how to properly hold a fork and spoon: not in a fist, but comfortably with the thumb and forefinger, about three-quarters of the way down the handle.

LEARN TO MAKE PLEASANT MEALTIME CONVERSATION. Do not criticize the food and do thank the hostess or cook upon finishing the meal.

ASK TO BE EXCUSED FROM THE TABLE. Children should be permitted to be excused from the table, when very young, if the meal is an extended one. Expecting a young child to sit quietly through a protracted meal when his food is gone is an unreasonable demand on his patience and ability to sit still without wiggling, fiddling, and noisemaking to help pass the time. "May I please be excused?" should be asked of parents or of the hostess when dining with friends and relatives.

Q. *How does one summon the waiter?*

A. In the United States, the usual way is to catch his eye and then raise your hand, first finger pointing up, as if to say "attention" or "listen." If he does not look in your direction you may call "Waiter" (or "Waitress") quietly, or if he is too far away to hear you, ask any other waiter nearby, "Please call our waiter." "Miss" is also a correct term for a waitress, but "Sir" is not correct for a waiter, whether used by a woman, man, or a youngster: "Waiter" is used instead.

Q. *Most restaurants serve more food than I can eat comfortably at one sitting. May I ask for a doggy bag to bring the food home?*

A. Certainly you may. It is perfectly acceptable if you are comfortable asking for one.

Q. *How do you complain about restaurant service? Do you speak with the server or ask for the manager?*

A. Complaints should be made quietly, without making a fuss or attracting the attention of other diners. They should be made first to the waiter (or the person who commits the error). If he or she makes no effort to correct the situation, the headwaiter or whomever is in charge of the dining room should be notified. Think twice when complaining about laziness or inattention, however, because difficulty in serving many people at once may not be the waiter's fault. Tables may be poorly allotted or the staff shorthanded, making it hard for your waiter to keep up with the requests of the patrons. Otherwise, any rudeness and inconsiderateness should be reported, as should dissatisfaction with the food.

On the other hand, appreciative comments are more than welcome and offered all too infrequently. If your meal and the service were excellent, it is extremely thoughtful to say so, both to the waiter and manager.

Q. *Does dining at a smorgasbord or buffet-style restaurant differ from dining at a restaurant with full table service?*

A. Yes, each is different in several aspects. At a smorgasbord restaurant, individual tables are set as usual, but the meal is not served by waiters. Instead it is set up as a buffet with stacks of small plates at one end to be filled with reasonable amounts of food. Since you are expected to make as many trips as you wish from your seat to the smorgasbord and back, you should never overload your plate and you should only choose foods that go well together each time you serve yourself. Leave your used plate and silver at your table for the waiter to remove while you are helping yourself to your next selection. Be sure to leave your waiter a tip.

Q. *Is is okay to eat from a cafeteria tray or should one take everything off the tray?*

A. You should take everything off the tray and place the tray in the receptacle it belongs in.

CHAPTER 9

CELEBRATIONS

Q. *What occasions call for formal third-person invitations? How is the invitation worded?*

A. The rule of thumb is that formal events require formal invitations. Occasions could include weddings, formal dinner parties, dances, receptions, teas, commencements, bar and bat mitzvahs, and any official, state, or diplomatic parties.

The invitation is worded in the third person. For example:

Mr. and Mrs. Robert Werner
request the pleasure of your company
at dinner
on Saturday, the ninth of September
at half past seven o'clock
Seabreeze
Seattle, Washington
RSVP
Box 636
Edgartown, Massachusetts 02539

Punctuation is used only when words requiring separation occur on the same line, and in certain abbreviations, such as "RSVP." The time should never be given as "nine-thirty," but as "half past nine o'clock," or the more conservative form, "half after nine o'clock." If the dance or dinner or other entertainment is to be given at one address and the hostess lives at another, both addresses are always given, assuming that the hostess wishes that replies go to her home address.

HOW IS THE REPLY TO A FORMAL INVITATION WORDED WHEN . . .

Q. . . . *you are accepting the invitation?*

A. The general rule is "reply-in-kind." The formal reply is written exactly as is the invitation, substituting the order of names. In accepting the invitation, you should repeat the day and hour so that any mistake can be rectified. If you decline an invitation, it is not necessary to repeat the hour.

If the invitation is like the formal one shown in the previous question, the acceptance reply would also be in the third person, such as:

Mr. and Mrs. Frank Kemp
accept with pleasure
the kind invitation of
Mr. and Mrs. Robert Werner
for dinner
on Saturday, the ninth of September
at half past seven o'clock

Q. . . . *you must decline the invitation?*

A.   Mr. and Mrs. Scott Dunn
                regret that they are unable to accept
                        the kind invitation of
                    Mr. and Mrs. Robert Werner
                for Saturday, the ninth of September

Q. *How far in advance of an occasion are invitations sent out?*

A. Depending on the type of occasion it is, invitations to large events are usually sent between four and six weeks ahead of time, and should be answered at once. If a party is held at a catering hall or restaurant, the caterer often wants to know the number of guests attending at least two weeks before the party, so prompt replies are essential. Wedding invitations are often sent up to eight weeks ahead, also for this reason.

Q. *Is it acceptable to extend invitations by telephone?*

A. Yes. Telephone invitations are correct for all but the most formal occasions.

Q. *How is a wedding invitation typically worded?*

A. The following wording is correct for weddings of any size:

Mr. and Mrs. Hunter Wilson
request the honour of your presence
at the marriage of their daughter
Catherine Elizabeth
to
Mr. Todd Campbell
Saturday, the fifth of April
half after four o'clock
Church of St. John the Divine
Minneapolis

Q. *How is a less formal invitation worded? How is the response worded?*

A. A less formal invitation may be a note, handwritten on an informal card. Also, it may be a purchased, fill-in invitation or one that is printed by using the formal, third-person format:

Mr. and Mrs. Arnold Davidson
request the pleasure of
Dr. and Mrs. Reid Coleman's
company at dinner
on Saturday, the second of March
at eight o'clock
44 High Street
Columbus, Ohio 43200
RSVP

The form of acceptance or regret depends upon the formality of the invitation received. If the RSVP information is a telephone number, then your response is made by telephone, if possible. If you are unable to reach the host by telephone, a note is always acceptable as long as it is prompt and there is time for it to be received well in advance of the day of the event. If the RSVP information is an address, a handwritten reply on your own informal stationery, or following the form of the included, fill-in invitation is expected.

Q. *I've been invited to a cocktail buffet that is being held the weekend my cousin is visiting. May I ask the hostess if my cousin may attend?*

A. No. When regretting an invitation because you have a guest yourself, you should explain your reason to the hostess. She then has the option to extend an invitation to your cousin or not.

Q. *Can I change my response to an invitation from yes to no?*

A. Yes, but it is important that you call the host as soon as possible, explain your problem, and express your regrets. Generally, extenuating circumstances are the only valid reasons for cancelling. If there is ample time, you may write, if you prefer, giving the reason and your apologies. In any event, it is essential that you let your host or hostess know right away.

Q. *. . . from no to yes?*

A. If the party to which you were originally invited is a large reception, a cocktail buffet, a picnic, or any gathering at which one or two extra guests would not cause a complication, you may call the hostess, explain that circumstances have changed, and ask if you may change your regret to an acceptance. If, however, the party involves a limited number of guests, such as a seated dinner, a theater party, or a bridge party, the hostess most likely has already filled your place.

Q. *What is a response card and how is it used?*

A. A response card is used to obtain a reply to an invitation. It is usually a small card that is printed in the same style as the invitation it accompanies. Response cards have a place for the invited guest to check whether he or she will attend or not. It is not a good idea to have a fill-in space for "number that will attend" since some recipients assume this means they may bring additional guests. Response cards that accompany invitations to private parties include a self-addressed, stamped envelope.

Q. *I received a wedding invitation that included a response card. I am unable to attend the wedding. May I write a note explaining my regret at not being able to attend rather than return the response card?*

A. You should use the card for your reply. The sender has likely organized a system for filing the returned cards, and a handwritten answer on notepaper would not fit in with the cards. You may, however, accompany the card with a handwritten note explaining your regret, so long as it is included with the card, and not in lieu of the card.

Q. *If an invitation is addressed to "Mr. and Mrs.," does it include their children?*

A. No, it does not. Only if the invitation is addressed "Mr. and Mrs. and family" or "and children," or if it lists the children's names after the adults' names, are the children included in the invitation.

Q. *May an unmarried person bring a guest to a wedding?*

A. Of course, but only if his or her invitation reads "and guest." If it does not, then the invitation is intended only for the person to whom it is addressed.

Q. *When I receive a wedding invitation addressed to me "and guest" do I tell the bride my guest's name when I respond?*

A. Yes, you should give her the name and address of your friend. Although it is not absolutely necessary, she may, at this time, send your guest an invitation. Even if she chooses not to, it is helpful to have your guest's name to prepare a placecard ahead of time.

Q. *How does a wedding announcement differ from an invitation?*

A. Announcements are just that—they announce that a wedding has taken place and are sent after the wedding. It is not mandatory to send wedding announcements, but they are useful as a means of informing old friends who have been out of touch, business associates, or people who live too far away to attend the wedding. Announcements are never sent to anyone who has received an invitation to the ceremony and/or the reception. Announcements should be sent as soon after the wedding as possible, preferably the next day. If there is an extenuating circumstance they may, however, be mailed up to several months later.

A wedding announcement may be worded as follows:

Mr. and Mrs. James Welch
have the honour of
announcing the marriage of their daughter
Christine Nicole
to
Mr. Thomas Charles Anders
Saturday, the twenty-seventh of March
One thousand nine hundred and ninety-seven
Washington, D.C.

Q. *What obligation does a wedding announcement carry?*

A. None, although a congratulatory note or card from the recipient to the couple is a thoughtful gesture. The receipt of an announcement does not mean that a gift must be sent in return. A gift may be sent, but it is not obligatory.

Q. *Who is invited to an engagement party? Are gifts brought to and opened at an engagement party?*

A. The guest list is unlimited, but the majority of engagement parties are restricted to relatives and good friends. Engagement gifts are not expected from ordinary friends and acquaintances. If gifts are given at all, they usually are given only by close relatives and very special friends, and they generally are given to the bride alone—not at the party. Sometimes they are given by the groom's family as a special welcome to the bride. Unless the custom in your family or your area is to bring gifts to the engagement party, in which case they are opened as part of the party, they should not be given at that time. It can cause embarrassment to the majority of the guests who have not brought anything. If guests do bring gifts, the bride should open them in private with only the donor present rather than making a display of them in front of those who did not bring anything. Or, if time does not permit this, they can be opened later with a prompt thank-you sent afterward.

Q. *Is there a set rule on who should and should not have bridal or baby showers for family members?*

A. Traditionally, the only people who have not been "eligible" to give showers are immediate family of the bride, groom, or mother-to-be. That generally means mothers, mothers-in-law, and sisters. Aunts, nieces, and cousins are not immediate family and may host a shower. There are exceptions to this no-immediate-family guideline, though, such as when the bride is from out of town and knows no one but members of her fiancé's immediate family.

Q. *We are having our first baby soon and want to send birth announcements but are afraid that people will think they are bids for gifts. Do birth announcements obligate the receivers to send a gift?*

A. No. Birth announcements carry no obligation. They do not mean that the recipients need send gifts. It is thoughtful, however, for those who receive announcements to send a note of congratulations to the new parents—and they certainly may send gifts if they wish.

Q. *Is there a standard form for birth announcement cards? Are birth announcements sent to local newspapers? If so, how would one be worded?*

A. No, there is no standard form. There is a large variety of commercially designed announcement cards available, as well as a large selection of announce-ments available through printers. Often parents design their own announcements, which can be the nicest cards of all. One type of birth announcement, and the most traditional, consists of a very small card with space for the baby's name and birthdate on it, tied with a pink or blue ribbon to the top of the "Mr. and Mrs." card of the parents.

Birth announcements are sometimes sent to news-papers. If so, they are usually sent the week following the birth, and their typical wording is: "Mr. and Mrs. Steven Krieger of 1009 Chesterfield Parkway, Colum-bus, announce the birth of a son, Benjamin, on July 2, 1995, at Doctor's Hospital. They have one daughter, Beth, three. Mrs. Krieger is the former Miss Barbara Dillon."

Q. *May we send birth announcements when we adopt a child?*

A. Most certainly. An announcement for an adopted child will bring reassuring comfort to the child later on, should he or she ever doubt his place in the hearts of the family who chose him.

Mr. and Mrs. Jason Black
have the happiness to announce
the adoption of
Courtney
age four months

If you choose to use a commercial birth announcement for your adopted child, choose one in which you can easily insert the words *adopted* or *adoption* and one appropriate to the child's age. In other words, don't select a card with a picture of a stork with a baby in its mouth to announce the arrival of a two-year-old. Some parents like to design their own adoption announcements.

Q. *Is it proper to have a shower for a friend who has adopted a baby?*

A. Of course it is! A shower for a new baby, up to one year old, is a wonderful welcome and affirmation of a newly formed family.

Q. *I have recently received invitations to baby showers for third and fourth children in a family. I am on a fixed income, and while I am very happy for these families, I really can't afford to participate in ongoing celebrations that require gifts. Have you any advice?*

A. A baby shower held for a first or even second child is fine, but it becomes an imposition to ask the same people to a third or fourth baby shower. However, you are not obligated to accept these invitations nor to send a gift if you do not go. Simply refuse politely, and send the prospective or new parents a congratulatory card. If you decide to accept, then you would take a gift.

Q. *How are invitations to a christening or* bris *issued?*

A. Usually, christening invitations are given over the telephone—or to out-of-towners, by personal note:

> Dear Annemarie and George,
> Julie will be christened on Sunday, the 23rd, at 3:00 pm in Christ Church. Would you come to the ceremony at the church, and join us afterward at our house?
> Love,
> Allison

Or a message may be written on the "Mr. and Mrs." cards of the parents or on an informal card, saying simply, "Julie's christening, Christ Church, March 23rd, 3 o'clock in the afternoon. Reception at our house afterward." All invitations to a christening are very friendly and informal.

For a *bris*, relatives and close friends are usually invited by telephone since the time between birth and the ceremony is short.

Q. *How should godparents be chosen?*

A. One asks a very intimate friend or relative to be a godparent, for it is a responsibility not to be undertaken lightly and also one difficult to refuse.

Q. *What are the obligations of a godparent toward their godchild?*

A. The obligation of being a godparent is essentially a spiritual one which recommends that the godparent be of the same faith as the parents. The godparent vows to see that the child is given religious training, learns the specific creeds and commandments of the church, and is confirmed at the proper time.

Beyond these obligations, he is expected to take a special interest in the child, much as a very close relative would do, remembering him or her with a gift on birthdays and on Christmas until the child is grown—or perhaps longer if they remain close.

Godparents who have lost contact with the child and his or her parents need not continue to give presents after the threads of friendship have broken.

Godparents do not have any obligation to give financial assistance or to assume the care of children who lose their parents. This responsibility is the guardian's—not the godparent's.

Q. *Who provides the christening outfit, the parents or the godparents?*

A. The parents do. The dress may be new or one that was worn by the baby's mother, father, or even one of his or her grandparents or great-grandparents. Usually everything the baby wears is white, although this is a custom, not a religious requirement.

Q. *Who hosts an anniversary party? May the couple host the party, or do family members do the planning?*

A. Early anniversary parties are usually given by the couple themselves. By the time they reach the twenty-fifth, they may well have grown children who wish to make the arrangements, but it is perfectly correct for them to do so themselves if their children do not or cannot. When a couple do not have children, close friends sometimes prepare the celebration. Fiftieth anniversary celebrations are almost invariably planned by the family of the couple.

Q. *What type of invitation is appropriate for an anniversary party?*

A. The form of the invitations depends entirely on the degree of formality of the party. They may range from an informal telephone call to an engraved third-person invitation. Formal invitations for a twenty-fifth anniversary are often bordered and printed in silver; those for a fiftieth, in gold. The most common forms are handwritten notes, or the necessary information written on an informal or fill-in card.

Q. *My husband and I are planning to reaffirm our wedding vows for our tenth anniversary. The service and reception will be held at our home with about 100 guests. We would prefer no gifts to us personally. Instead we would like to enclose a separate card in the invitation stating that the traditional gift of ten years is tin/aluminum and that a basket will be provided for donations of canned goods to an organization that feeds*

*the hungry. We don't know how to word the card with-
out sounding as if we assumed people were planning on
giving us gifts. We want to tie traditional ideas with a
modern need without offending would-be guests. Can
you help?*

A. You can be sure that people would expect to bring
you a gift on your tenth anniversary, so don't worry
about that. Enclose a card, or write on the invitation,
"In lieu of a 10th anniversary gift of tin or aluminum,
we invite you to contribute to a basket of canned food
to be sent to World Hunger Relief" (or "to our local
food pantry for the homeless and hungry"). There
would be less hunger in the world if there were more
people like you!

Q. *When graduation draws near, I will be very proud to
send graduation announcements to relatives, but how
do I know which of my friends, my parents' friends, or
friends of the family to send announcements to without
making it look as if I am showing off or expecting a
gift? Do I send announcements to those friends of the
family or my parents' friends whose children have never
sent graduation announcements to my family?*

A. Graduation announcements serve the purpose of
advising close friends and relatives of your exciting
news. The recipients of announcements are not
obliged to send you gifts, and you needn't worry
about "showing off"—those close to you will be

happy for you. There is no set formula regarding who among family and parents' friends to send announcements to. You needn't send many announcements, but do send them to those who would really like to know of your accomplishment.

Q. *My son is a senior in high school and will be graduating in the spring. I would like to send graduation announcements to a few select friends and relatives without them thinking they must send money or a gift. Would it be appropriate to include a note "no gifts"?*

A. Announcements do not carry any obligation, but many people do not know that and feel they must send a gift. Either send the announcements to very close friends and relatives who would want and expect to send a gift, or have "no gifts please" written on the announcements if you are adamant about this point.

Q. *Is it okay to give our own housewarming party?*

A. Yes, it's a great way of showing your new house to friends. When you have put a lot of time and effort into making a home that's yours, you are naturally as eager to share it with your friends as they are to see it. A housewarming is generally a cocktail party or a cocktail buffet. It may be as simple or as elaborate as you wish.

Q. *Some very close friends are moving away and I would like to have a farewell party for them. Is this appropriate? Should people bring gifts?*

A. It is perfectly appropriate. It's a good idea to coordinate your plans with other friends so that the guests of honor are not exhausted by several farewell parties. There's a story about a popular couple moving to a new town who were fêted to some thirteen farewell parties! By the time the departure date arrived, their exhausted friends could hardly wait for them to go. Friends are expected to take farewell gifts to a party, but if there is one particular gift that would be too expensive for individuals to give, you could coordinate its purchase, requesting a reasonable contribution from the guests who are able to attend. This should be noted on the invitation—"We will be giving John and Mary a watercolor of their house here, as a gift from all of us. A contribution to Jean Gould, 10 Adams Street, would be appreciated. Your name will be signed on the card that will accompany the gift." This indicates that the gift is taken care of, and delegating the collection toward it to another friend frees the hostess to plan the party.

Q. *Should I give a retirement party for my father, for our family and friends to attend?*

A. Retirement parties are usually given by professional associates, but relatives or close friends may certainly give a party, too.

Q. *Suddenly, birthday parties for adult friends are being given. Is this socially correct?*

A. Certainly! There is no limit on the kind of celebration this may be, from a barbecue or picnic to a formal dinner dance at a club or restaurant. The only real requirement is that at some point during the party, the host or hostess asks for the attention of the assembled guests and offers a toast to the birthday person. Often guests wish to make their own toasts, read a poem or verse prepared especially for the guest of honor, or make a speech about the birthday person. Invitations may be preprinted, fill-in, or even telephone calls, depending on the formality of the event. Because it is a birthday party, it is assumed that gifts are to be taken, unless the invitation indicates "no gifts, please." The guest of honor may elect to open the gifts during or after the party, depending on its formality and size, and other activities may occur during the party.

Q. *Do you think that children should open birthday gifts at their birthday parties?*

A. Yes, I do. I know that some parents don't trust that their child won't say, "I already have this!" or "I hate this present," not meaning to be insensitive, but because they are basically honest and blunt. Other parents don't want the guests at the party taking gifts and using them before the birthday child has a chance to play with them. Both these situations are readily resolved and provide an important opportunity for parents to teach their children about basic sensitivity and sharing with others.

Parents should help a child prepare for what to say when a duplicate gift is received, or when they open something they don't like or can't use. A small child can be told that it might hurt a friend's feelings to announce that he already has something he receives as a gift, or that if he receives the same game or toy from two friends he can say how great it is because that means more people can play with them at the same time. He should be told that it is important to exclaim, "Thank you!" when he opens a gift, even if he doesn't like it. When children are small and want immediately to play with gifts as they are opened, it is important for an adult to set gifts aside, after they have been admired, with a comment that Becky may want a chance to look at all her presents again before they are used by anybody else. Then, after the gift-opening part of the party, she can play with some of her gifts with her friends.

Q. *Do you have any advice for a way to keep children at a large party from all crowding around the birthday child as she opens her gifts?*

A. A very nice way to handle this is to place the birthday child in a large chair and have each guest present his gift and sit next to the birthday child as the card is read and the gift is opened. This gives special attention to each guest, and lets all the children know that they will have a turn to be close to the birthday child. Make it clear that the guest returns to the circle after his present is opened, to make room for the next person.

Q. *My parents are divorced and unfriendly to each other. I am at a loss to know how to include everyone in special events such as my children's birthdays and holidays. How do I know which one to invite? When they both invite us for the same holiday, what do I do so that I don't hurt either one's feelings? They make me feel as if I'm abandoning them if I don't accept both. We also have my husband's parents to consider.*

A. Your sensitivity is admirable, but your priority is with your own family and the creation of holiday traditions that will become your children's own. You cannot make your parents' hostile relationship your problem. Be frank with each, telling them that you want special times to be relaxed and happy for your children. This means that you cannot spend Christmas, for example, traveling to one's home and then the other's, and then to your husband's parents. Consider taking turns celebrating an event on its real date with one, and then have a second celebration on another day with the other. Another option is to alternate having each parent join you at your own home.

Do not allow them to put you in the middle. Remind them that you love them both, but insist that your children be able to spend time with all their grandparents in peace, happiness, and harmony.

Assuming that both your parents are otherwise gracious people, think about having each of them take turns joining you and your in-laws at some of the holiday celebrations.

For those once-in-a-lifetime events that cannot be duplicated (a christening, graduation, recital, or wedding) ask your parents if, for the sake of their grandchildren, they couldn't "bury the hatchet" for that day so both could be present.

Q. *Some of my neighbors are Jewish, but speak often of Christmas as though they celebrate it somewhat. When they wish me a very Merry Christmas would it be appropriate for me to say "and the same to you"?*

A. Rather than responding this way, say, "And a Happy Hanukkah to you." They are respecting your faith, and you'll be showing respect for theirs in return when you acknowledge their celebrations.

Q. *Is there a way to tactfully decline a request that you serve in a position of honor, such as a bridesmaid or godparent? Sometimes people presume a friendship is deeper than it is, and considering the responsibility and the cost, it can be a lot to ask.*

A. If the money is a problem, simply tell the truth. Say, "I would like nothing better than to be in your wedding, but my money situation is so tight that I'm afraid I'll have to decline." If you find the responsibility of being a godparent or guardian daunting, tactfully say so. The new parents will appreciate your honesty.

Q. *Is is alright to ask for a doggy bag at a wedding or other catered party if I can't finish what I have been served?*

A. No. It is okay to do so in a restaurant, when you are paying for your food, but not at a wedding reception, where you are the guest of someone else.

Q. *I am planning a cocktail party buffet. How can I accommodate both meat eaters and vegetarians?*

A. By planning wisely, you can easily accommodate both groups. Make sure you provide one hearty main dish each for both vegetarians and meat eaters. Supplement these main dishes with vegetable salads, pasta salads, and vegetable crudités. Some vegetarians will eat eggs and milk products, such as cheese; inquire beforehand and then plan your buffet around these as main dishes, with vegetables on the side. Offer both a meat and a vegetarian appetizer.

CHAPTER 10

GIFTS

Q. *When is it acceptable to give money as a gift?*

A. Some ethnic groups traditionally give money as wedding gifts, and today, in general, more and more couples are receiving gift certificates and checks as wedding presents. Often money is given for a religious confirmation, a first communion, a bar or bat mitzvah, and a graduation. Another occasion for which a gift of money is appropriate is a fiftieth wedding anniversary. Many older couples, perhaps living on a pension or social security, may appreciate cash more than gifts, which they neither need nor have room for.

For people who dislike the idea of giving a check or cash, a gift certificate is a good compromise.

Q. *We have received invitations to birthday and anniversary parties that state "No Gifts Please." Does this also include gifts of money? I never know what to do.*

A. When an invitation says "no gifts please," it means just that—no gifts, money or otherwise, should be brought to the party. Ignoring the request would only serve to embarrass the host and the other guests. If someone does choose to bring a gift, then it should not be opened during the party or put on display. The gift can be opened at a later time, in private, and the donor thanked by note.

Q. *Should gifts be opened at a party?*

A. Yes. Half the fun of giving and receiving presents at any party is to see and enjoy what everyone else brought. The best way to do this is to have all the presents collected in one place until everyone has arrived, at which time the guest of honor opens them. The recipient reads the cards enclosed. If someone has given money instead of a present, the amount should not be mentioned. On occasions when someone brings a gift when gifts are not expected, the present is opened in the donor's presence alone. This might happen, for instance, when a couple brings a gift to a dinner hostess.

Q. *How can you respond when someone arrives with an unexpected gift at Christmastime?*

A. Unless you have a supply of small gifts or tins of home-baked goods ready for such an emergency, you can only say, "Thanks so much—but you shouldn't have done this," to indicate that you do not expect to start an annual exchange of gifts.

Q. *Which is better—to send flowers to your hosts before or after a party?*

A. When a party is given especially for you, it's preferable to send flowers to your hostess beforehand. Otherwise, flowers sent later as a thank-you for a great time are always appreciated.

Q. *Should guests bring gifts of food or wine to their hosts?*

A. If it is the custom in your part of the country to take a gift to a small dinner party, by all means do so. For a large or formal party, however, it is better not to take a gift at all, especially if you do not know the hosts well. It will only embarrass other guests who have not brought a gift. In general, follow the custom of the area.

The custom of taking wine as a gift to a dinner party is becoming a popular one. Not too expensive or elaborate, wine can be enjoyed right away or put away for another evening. A guest who takes a gift of food to a dinner party should not expect it to be served as part of the meal, unless the hostess has been consulted first. A hostess who has planned a dessert, say, to complement her meal, should never be made to feel she must also serve another. A box of candy or croissants and jam for the hosts' breakfast the next morning is a thoughtful gift and can alleviate any confusion about when to serve it.

Q. *What gifts are returned when an engagement is broken? Are wedding gifts returned if the marriage lasts only a short time?*

A. All gifts except those that are monogrammed should be returned if an engagement is broken, including the engagement ring and any gifts of value received from the fiancé or fiancée. Shower gifts, too, should be returned if the marriage is called off. Once the wedding has taken place, however, gifts are not returned, no matter how short-lived the marriage, unless the wedding is annulled before the couple lives together.

Q. *What do I do if a gift arrives broken?*

A. If it arrives directly from a local store, take it with its wrappings to the shop where it was purchased. If it comes from another city or a mail-order company, return it by mail, accompanied by a letter explaining how it arrived. Any reputable store or company will happily replace the merchandise if it was received in a damaged condition. You don't have to involve the donor in this or even let her know what happened. If the package was packed and mailed by the donor, not a store, and it was insured, you must let the sender know so she can collect the insurance and replace the gift. If the package was not insured, it is best not to mention the damaged condition, since the sender will feel obligated to replace the gift at his own, duplicate expense.

Q. *May duplicate wedding gifts be exchanged? Do I need to tell the donor?*

A. Yes, duplicate wedding gifts may be exchanged, so long as they are not from close family members, unless they suggest that the bride exchange the gift. When a duplicate gift is received from someone who lives far away, the couple need not mention the fact that they are exchanging a present on their thank-you note. It is wise, however, to explain the exchange to anyone who will be visiting your house. If you do mention the exchange to the donor, it is important to mention in your thank-you note that you are enjoying what you got as a replacement, thanks to them.

Q. *When and where are wedding gifts delivered? Are gifts brought to a wedding reception?*

A. Gifts are generally delivered to the bride's home before the day of the wedding. They may be delivered in person or sent directly from the store where they were purchased. In some localities and among certain ethnic groups it is customary to take your gift to the wedding reception rather than send it ahead of time. In this instance, checks are usually handed to the bride and groom in the receiving line, but gift packages are placed on a table set up for just that purpose. If there is a large number of presents, the bride and groom do not open them until a later date.

THANK-YOU NOTES

OCCASION	OBLIGATION
Dinner parties	Only if you are a guest of honor.
Overnight	Always, except in the case of visits to close friends or relatives whom you see frequently. Then, a telephone call would serve the purpose.
Birthdays, Anniversary, Christmas, etc.	Always, when you have not thanked the donor in person. An exception: A phone call to a very close friend or relative is sufficient.
Shower gifts	If the donor was not at the shower or you did not extend verbal thanks.
Gifts to a sick person	Notes to out-of-towners and calls or notes to close friends are obligatory as soon as the patient feels well enough.

Condolence	Thank-yous should be sent for all condolence notes, except for printed cards with no personal message.
Congratulatory	All personal messages or gifts must be acknowledged.
Wedding gifts	Obligatory—even though verbal thanks have been given. All wedding gifts must be acknowledged within three months, but preferably as the gifts arrive.
Hostess Gifts	Even though the gift is a thank-you itself, the hostess must thank her visitors, especially if the gift has arrived by mail, so that the visitor will know it has been received.

Q. *How soon after receiving a gift should the thank-you note be written?*

A. Thank-you notes should be written promptly, particularly when a gift is received through the mail or a delivery service and the donor has no way of knowing if you received it or not. Although it is preferable that the bride and groom acknowledge all gifts as they are received, they may, if necessary, take up to three months, at the outside, to send their thank-yous.

Q. *What should I do when I don't receive any acknowledgment for a gift?*

A. If you delivered the gift in person and the gift wasn't opened in your presence, you know it was received and that the recipient is simply exercising bad manners. If, however, you mailed the gift or had it sent from a store and have received no acknowledgment after three months at the outside, you may write and ask whether or not it was received. If your letter embarrasses the recipient, so be it. It is inexcusable not to thank the donor for a gift.

One suggestion: Send all gifts insured. You then have a good reason to write and say, "Since I haven't heard from you, I assume the gift I sent was lost. If that is so, I would like to put a claim in for the insurance, so would you let me know as soon as possible whether you received it or not."

When the gift in question is a check, you might write, "I am concerned about the check I sent you for your birthday. It has been cashed and returned to me, but since I have received no word from you, I am worried that it fell into the wrong hands and it was not you who cashed it. Would you please let me know?"

Q. *Who writes the thank-you notes, the bride or the groom? How are they signed, with only the bride's or groom's name, or with both names?*

A. Since most gifts are sent to the bride, she usually

writes and signs the thank-you note, but there is no reason the groom should not share this task. It is not incorrect to sign both names, but it is preferable to sign only one name and include the other in the text: "Bob and I are so delighted with . . . etc." or "Jean and I . . . etc."

Q. *I have a friend who gives me a gift every birthday, and this makes me feel uncomfortable because we aren't really that close. How can I put an end to this practice without being rude?*

A. One way is by not reciprocating; that way you send the message that exchanging birthday gifts with your friend is not required. Even so, thank her for the present and say, "You really shouldn't have." Another way to stop her gift-giving is to be tactful, yet direct, in telling her that you've appreciated her gifts but feel the two of you should cut back and send each other birthday cards instead. You can say you've cut back on all your personal gift giving; you can add a reason (your budget, your time restraints). You needn't single her out by saying you're not close enough (which would be hurtful, to say the least!). Instead let her know that in general you're involved in fewer gift exchanges.

Q. *My fiancé and I aren't interested in traditional wedding china or silver. We'd much rather have friends and family help us out with a great honeymoon trip. Would it be tacky to suggest this?*

A. No, not if the suggestion is made when people ask for ideas—and if you let them *choose* this gift from various options on your wish list. Many couples are choosing nontraditional wedding gifts, such as a down payment on a house, recreational equipment, and home appliances. Gift registries for engaged couples have opened up in home and garden centers, recreational outfitters, and computer stores. A "honeymoon fund" may be set up by a close family member, who can then spread the word regarding the wishes of the engaged couple. Details about gift registries should never be included on a wedding invitation.

CHAPTER 11

GRIEVING AND CONDOLENCES

Q. *When and how are calls of condolence made?*

A. They should be made as soon as possible after hearing of the death, especially if the friends suffering the loss are close ones, in which case you should offer your services to help in any way you can. There are countless ways to be helpful, from preparing food or assisting with child care to making phone calls or answering the door. You can help organize food if a gathering of family and friends is planned for after the funeral. You can offer to stay at the house during the funeral service (sometimes houses are robbed during a funeral when it is known that no one will be at home), or offer to be in charge of flowers, collecting all the accompanying cards one hour before the service and writing a description of the flowers or other gifts so the family can properly thank the giver at a later time. You can also offer to have out-of-town relatives attending the funeral stay at your home, or offer to drive family members to and from the funeral home or the church or synagogue, or to run other errands.

If, on the other hand, your friends do not need

anything, don't linger; offer your sympathy and leave without delay.

A condolence call to a Jewish family is made during the seven days following the burial. This period of mourning is known as sitting *shivah* (*shivah* is the Hebrew word for seven). A call made to the home of those in mourning gives you an opportunity to express your sympathy to the bereaved.

When you are not closely acquainted with the family and do not wish to intrude on their privacy, simply leave or mail a condolence card.

When you are making a condolence call at a funeral home, sign the register, a record of visitors who have come to pay their respect. If the family is not there to receive your sympathy in person, you should send a condolence at once. You may certainly telephone, but first consider the inconvenience it may cause in tying up the line.

Q. *How should relatives be notified of a death?*

A. Members of the family and other close friends should be called on the telephone. Other relatives, even those who live at some distance, should also be called, but if expense is a factor, friends who live far away and who would not be expected to attend the funeral or memorial service may be notified by letter.

Q. *How is a newspaper notice of death worded?*

A. Newspaper notices usually contain the date of death, the names of the immediate family, the hours and locations where friends may call on the family, the place and time of the funeral, and frequently, a request that a contribution be given to a charity in lieu of flowers.

Often, the cause of death is included. The word *suddenly* is sometimes inserted to indicate that there had not been a long illness or that the death was an accident. Often "after a long illness" is included to communicate that information. The deceased's age may or may not be included.

Daughters of the deceased are listed before sons. A married woman's notice includes her given and maiden name for purposes of identification. The same is true when married daughters and sisters are mentioned. The use of adjectives such as *beloved*, *loving*, or *devoted* is optional.

A woman's notice might read:

Cohen—Helen Weinberg, on May 13. [Beloved] wife of Isaac, [loving] mother of Rebecca, Paul, and Samuel, [devoted] sister of Anna Weinberg Gold and Paul Weinberg. Services Thursday, May 14, 2:00 P.M., at Star Funeral Home, 41 Chestnut Street, Pittsburgh. In lieu of flowers, contributions may be sent to the United Jewish Appeal, or your favorite charity.

A man's notice might read:

Johnson—Michael B., on December 12, 1988. [Beloved] husband of the late Kathleen Stuart Johnson. [Devoted] father of Erin Johnson Flynn, Brad S., and Sean R. Friends may call at 44 Wendt Avenue, Harrison, New York, on Friday, December 15, 2–5. Funeral service Saturday, December 16, 11:30 A.M., St. John's Lutheran Church, Mamaroneck, New York.

An obituary may also be run in the newspaper, often submitted by the family. It is the option of the newspaper editors to decide whether to print it or not. In the event that one is submitted, it generally includes the residence of family members listed (Brad S. of New York City, Sean R. of Mamaroneck) and information about the deceased's career, previous activities, and memberships and affiliations. If the person who died was prominent in the community, it is probable that the newspapers already have a file on him or her. Still, the information on file should be checked by someone who was close to the deceased so that no errors are made in the published obituary.

Q. *What does "in lieu of flowers" mean?*

A. It means that the family requests a contribution to a specific charity instead of a condolence gift of flowers. A check is then sent to the charity, accompanied by a note saying that the donation was sent in memory of the deceased. Your address, as well as the deceased's family's, should appear on the note. If no "in lieu of" appears in the notice, you should send flowers.

Occasionally a notice reads, "Please send a contribution to your favorite charity." The amount of the contribution is up to you. Don't, however, give less than you would have paid for a flower arrangement.

Another option: Send a plant or flower arrangement to the family a few days after the funeral as an indication of your continuing sympathy and love. Cards accompanying these flowers or plants should not mention the recent loss, but may simply say, "With love from us all," or "With love."

Q. *Who generally serve as pallbearers? May someone refuse to serve as a pallbearer?*

A. Generally, close male friends of the deceased serve as pallbearers. They may be asked when they come to pay their respects or by telephone. Members of the immediate family are never chosen, as their place is with the family.

One cannot refuse an invitation to be a pallbearer except for illness or absence from the area.

Q. *What are honorary pallbearers and what role do they play in a funeral?*

A. Honorary pallbearers serve only at church funerals. They do not carry the coffin. This service is performed by the assistants of the funeral director, who are expertly trained. The honorary pallbearers sit in the first pews on the left, and after the service leave the church two by two, walking immediately in front of the coffin.

Q. *Who serves as ushers at a funeral or memorial service, and what do they do?*

A. Ushers may be chosen in addition to, or in place of, pallbearers. Although funeral directors will supply men to perform the task, it is infinitely better to select men from the family (not immediate family), or good friends, who will recognize those who come and seat them according to their closeness to the family or according to their own wishes. At both a funeral and a memorial service, ushers hand those who enter a bulletin of the service, if one is used, and show them to a pew. They walk slightly ahead of women guests and do not offer their arms unless someone needs assistance. At a memorial service, they ask people to sign a register, if the family wishes, before entering. When there are no pallbearers, the ushers sit in the front pews on the left and exit ahead of the coffin as pallbearers would. If there are pallbearers, the ushers remain at the back of the church.

Q. *If you extend an expression of sympathy at a funeral home, do you also write a condolence note?*

A. A visitor who sees and personally extends his sympathy at the funeral home need not write a note of condolence, but he may if he wants to, particularly if he wishes to write an absent member of the family. Those who merely sign the register and do not speak with family members should, in addition, write a note.

Q. *Who may stop by a funeral home to pay his respects? Who attends a funeral?*

A. Anyone who wishes to express his sympathy to the family of the deceased may stop by a funeral home and pay his respects. People who do not feel they are close enough to intrude on the privacy of the bereaved may stop in at times other than those during which the family is there and sign the register.

If the newspaper notice reads "Funeral private," only those who have received an invitation from the family may go. If the hour and the location of the service are printed in the paper, that is considered an invitation to anyone who wishes to attend.

A divorced man or woman should go to the funeral of their former spouse if the latter had not remarried and there are children involved. Even if the deceased had remarried, the former spouse should only attend if cordial relations have been maintained with the family of the deceased, and then he or she should sit in the rear and not attempt to join the family. If the deceased had remarried and ill will still existed between the divorced couple, the former spouse should not attend but should send flowers and a brief note of condolence.

Q. *Can you give me some guidance on what to do when paying my respects at a funeral home?*

A. When there is a coffin present, and if you feel comfortable in doing so, go forward to the coffin to say a prayer, either standing in front of it or kneeling on the kneeling bench that is generally provided. Don't stay by the coffin for a protracted period of time if there are others waiting in line, nor should you rush past. Don't leave without expressing your sympathy to close family members. Then sign the register provided and depart. You may sit quietly in chairs provided to meditate or reflect. If, as is often the case, there is active conversation among other visitors and you are seeing old friends and family members whom you have not seen for a long period, there is nothing wrong with greeting them and speaking quietly. No matter how social the gathering becomes, you should never tell jokes or talk loudly. When you depart, you may again approach the coffin to say a prayer, but you do not need to say good-bye to the family members to whom you have already spoken.

Q. *Can a funeral service be held at a funeral home rather than at a church?*

A. Yes, it can. This occurs most often when the deceased has not had a particular religious affiliation.

Q. *I recently attended a funeral for a person I did not personally know but whose family I wanted to support.*

At the end of the funeral I wasn't sure if I should walk past the casket or not—what should I have done?

A. Even though you did not know the deceased, it is still a sign of respect to walk past the casket when your turn comes.

Q. *Does everyone wear black when attending a funeral?*

A. No, it is no longer considered necessary to wear black unless you sit with the family or have been asked to be one of the honorary pallbearers. You should, however, wear clothes that are subdued in color and inconspicuous. On no account should children be put into black at any time. They should wear their best conservative clothes to a funeral.

Q. *Does everyone who attends a funeral also attend the burial?*

A. Only if the burial is in the churchyard or within walking distance of the church—and the congregation has been invited to the burial—does the congregation follow the family to the graveside. Otherwise, those attending the funeral, wherever the services are held, do not go to the interment unless they are family members or close friends, or unless the funeral director makes a general announcement about how cars will form a processional outside, which indicates that anyone who wishes to continue on should do so.

Q. *What is a memorial service? How does it differ from a funeral? Does a memorial service replace a funeral service?*

A. A memorial service takes the place of a funeral. It is held after the deceased has been buried or cremated privately, or when the deceased has died in another country, or perhaps in an airplane accident or accident at sea. If it takes place shortly after the death, the service is very much like a funeral service. If it takes place much later, however, it is more often very brief. In general the outline of the service is as follows: Two verses of a hymn are sung, short prayers follow, and a very brief address is given about the work and life of the one for whom the service is held. It is closed with a prayer and a verse or two of another hymn. Usually no flowers are sent except those for the altar.

An alternative to a memorial service is a "Service of Thanksgiving for the Life of (John Doe)." The service is simple, consisting of two or three tributes or eulogies given by friends or relatives, a prayer by the clergyman or clergywoman, and perhaps two or three hymns or musical offerings that were favorites of the deceased.

Q. *Is it proper to have a receiving line after a memorial service?*

A. Yes, it is. Since there generally are no formal visiting hours at a funeral home when a memorial service rather than an immediate funeral is held, a receiving line affords those who attend the service the chance to express their sympathy to family members.

Q. *What is the purpose of a reception after a memorial service or funeral? Those I have attended have seemed like parties and I think this is inappropriate. Do you agree?*

A. As long as the reception does not turn into a raucous affair, I see nothing wrong with this practice. It serves the purpose of giving friends and family the opportunity to gather, share their memories, and give support and love to one another.

Q. *Where should a reception after a funeral or memorial service be held?*

A. A reception may be held in the hall of the church. If this is the case, the minister should be asked to invite all present to the hall following the service. Generally, coffee and cakes are served, and, if a formal receiving line is not held at the back of the church, one may be formed in the hall so that mourners may speak to each family member. A reception may also be held in the home of the spouse or children of the deceased, or at the home of a close friend or other family member. If the host has the space and wishes to extend an invitation to all present, again the minister would announce this during the service. If space is limited and the reception is for only some of the guests, then one of the family members in the receiving line would say, "Please come back to the house with us, afterward." In this case, a friend or caterer has remained at the host house to prepare for guests. Usually an informal buffet is provided, along with beverages.

Q. *How does a family acknowledge expressions of sympathy?*

A. Flowers, messages, Mass cards, personal condolences, contributions, and special kindnesses must all be acknowledged. Printed condolence cards with no personal message added and calls at the funeral home need not be acknowledged. A personal message on a fold-over card is the preferable form for acknowledging expressions of sympathy. The note may be brief, but should be warm and mention the specific kindness or floral arrangement. Printed or engraved cards may also be used, as long as a personal handwritten note is added to the printed message. If the condolences have come from strangers, however, as is often the case when a public figure or a member of his family dies and hundreds of impersonal messages are received, an engraved or printed card need not include a handwritten addition. Printed cards usually read:

The family of
Harrison L. Winthrop
wishes to thank you for
your kind expression of sympathy

If the list of personal acknowledgments to be sent is a long one, or if the person who has received the flowers and messages is unable to perform the task of writing, a member of the family or a near friend may write for him or her.

Letters must also be written to honorary pallbearers and ushers, thanking them for their service, noting how much their presence meant to the family.

Q. *Several months ago my eighty-seven-year-old grandfather died. When people heard the news and told me, "I'm sorry," I was unsure how to respond. "Thank you" didn't seem right. What would be the appropriate response?*

A. There are several ways of responding to "I'm sorry." You might say, "Yes, we are going to miss him so much," or "I really appreciate your sympathy," or "Yes, he was a wonderful person, wasn't he?"

Q. *Who should attend a funeral of a business associate?*

A. If the funeral is not private, anyone who worked closely with the deceased should attend the funeral, even though he or she may not know any of the family members personally.

Q. *Is it proper to e-mail friends and relatives to let them know about someone's passing?*

A. Only if the friend or relative was not particularly

close to the deceased, or if you are sending the message to people who live far away.

Q. *Several of my friends have had miscarriages. Is it proper to send a sympathy card in this instance? What do I do or say?*

A. It is fine to send a sympathy card, or to say how sorry you are that this happened. Simply express your condolences and ask if there is anything you can do; never say anything such as: "Oh, you'll get pregnant again in no time!" or "It's all for the best."

Q. *I am amazed at the gall of people who show up at funeral homes for open casket viewings who were not close to the deceased. My mother just died, and several of these people were there for the viewing. Would it have been rude for me to ask them to leave?*

A. Yes, since they were likely there to show their support and respect for members of the remaining family. Your best approach would have been to simply thank them for coming.

Q. *My husband just passed away. Can I still wear my wedding ring?*

A. Absolutely. Wear it for as long as you wish. If you do remarry someday, you would then remove it.

Q. *Is is proper to bring small children to funerals or to funeral-home viewings?*

A. Traditions vary from culture to culture. In general, however, it is inappropriate to bring small children to funerals, unless the decased was a very close relative. Funeral-home viewings are generally off limits to young children.

CHAPTER 12

AT TIMES OF WORSHIP

Q. *Is it proper to ask a priest for his blessing, perhaps as you are about to leave his company? May a person of another faith ask for a priest's blessing?*

A. It is perfectly correct for a Catholic to ask for a Catholic priest's blessing. It is also permissible for other Christians to ask for a blessing if they wish.

Q. *My neighbor, who is Jewish, has asked me to attend services with her and then attend a Passover Seder. I would love to do this, but I am clueless as to what is expected of me and what I could offer toward the Seder, and don't want to appear rude out of ignorance. What should I do?*

A. It cannot be said enough times that clear communication is one of the basic tenets on which etiquette is based. Just ask her. Tell her how much you are looking forward to joining her and learning more about her faith and customs, but that you don't know what to do. Ask what you could bring to the Seder and what you could read or study ahead of time to help you participate more fully. This is not impolite, but shows genuine interest and caring.

Q. *Some close family members have recently converted to a different religion and they are determined to convert us, too. This is making family get-togethers prickly and uncomfortable. We are perfectly happy with our religious affiliation, feel just as religious as they do, and resent their constant attempts to proselytize and implications that we will not be "saved" until we join them in their new church. We hate to sever the relationship since our family isn't all that big to begin with, but just what can we say without being outright rude?*

A. There is no one as dedicated as a recent convert, so you must be just as emphatic as your relatives in stating that you are happy with your affiliation. Say that you respect their choice and are happy for them, and that you expect the same respect from them. If their zeal continues, you must say that you have listened to them and appreciate their strong feelings, but that you are not the least bit interested in converting. Tell them you are interested in maintaining a close relationship, and hope they will help keep these ties strong by expressing interest in other aspects of your lives and theirs.

Q. *How should you dress for a service at a church? a synagogue?*

A. Although clothing restrictions have been greatly relaxed in recent years, the correct dress is still conservative. Even today skirts or conservative pants and jackets for women and suits, slacks, and shirts and/or sport jackets for men are preferable to jeans or shorts for conventional church or synagogue services.

Hats for women are no longer required in most Christian churches, but are always correct. In Orthodox Jewish tradition, married women are required to wear a head covering (both in and out of synagogues).

Men never wear head coverings in Christian churches—they always do in synagogues. If you are not Jewish and are attending a synagogue for a service, a wedding, or a funeral, there are extra yarmulkes by the entrance. Although it is not your faith or practice, it is expected that you wear a yarmulke when attending any type of Jewish religious service.

Q. *Do ushers escort everyone to their seats in church?*

A. Not necessarily. Often ushers simply greet worshipers as they enter and then let them seat themselves. If the ushers do seat members of the congregation, they escort them to a pew. A woman does not take the usher's arm unless she needs assistance, but rather follows him as he leads the way to a vacant seat. The usher stands aside while the arrival—whether single or a couple—steps in. Women precede their husbands into the pew, going in far enough to allow room for him, and for children or others who are with them. At a special service, such as a wedding or first communion, early arrivals may keep their aisle seats, standing to let later arrivals get past them. At weekly services, however, those who are already in the pews should move over to make room for later arrivals.

Q. *Is it acceptable to stop and chat or wave to friends before services begin?*

A. It is perfectly correct to nod, smile, or wave at acquaintances before a service starts, and if a friend sits down next to you or in front of you, you may certainly lean over and whisper "Hello." You should not, however, chat, carry on a prolonged conversation, or introduce people to one another until after the service.

Q. *If you decide to attend another place of worship on a regular basis do you owe the clergyperson an explanation?*

A. Yes, you owe the clergyperson of your former church or synagogue an explanation, both for record-keeping and personal reasons. In some denominations, each parish is assessed for the national organization according to the number of registered members, and therefore its financial condition can be harmed if a member who leaves is still enrolled but not contributing.

You owe the clergyperson a personal explanation of your reasons for leaving, either by letter or in person. Although it may be difficult, try to be very honest and clear. While he or she may be hurt or upset, your comments may help him to serve the congregation better.

Q. *To me, any house of worship should be a place of quiet for meditation and prayer. There are a few families in my church who appear to be oblivious to their children and let them talk, thump their feet against the pew, and play with noisy toys. I went up to them one morning and asked them to keep their children quiet. They were quite offended and don't come to church anymore. The minister is annoyed with me. Was I wrong?*

A. You are correct that it is inconsiderate of parents to permit their children to disrupt an entire congregation's attempt to worship. A different way to handle this situation would be to make an appointment to speak with the minister and ask him or her to speak privately to the parents about the problem of noise and disruption. Many churches offer a nursery or "cry room" during worship for just this reason. It is difficult for small children to remain quiet for the length of time most services take, and a nursery allows them more freedom to release some of their energy. It is the minister's responsibility to periodically announce that nursery service is available and to remind parents that while the church loves to have its children present, it would be appreciated if parents would take them outside or to the nursery when they become noisy during worship.

Q. *Last week I made the mistake of again sitting in front of two women who talk through the entire service. The first time I just sat and seethed and tried to tune them out. This time I turned around and glowered at them. They now are not speaking to me. What should I have done?*

A. You did not do anything wrong in confronting them with their thoughtlessness and rudeness by your look. You might initiate a conversation with them outside of the sanctuary, however, to say that you are sorry you annoyed them, but that you have very sensitive hearing and found their talking distracting. This is about all you can politely say, since a lecture or more direct criticism would serve no better purpose than a quiet comment and probably would not be well received. Naturally, you will take care not to sit near them in the future and will endeavor to be pleasant and friendly when you see them.

Q. *I occasionally attend church with a friend of another faith. Do I participate in the service?*

A. Unless some part of the service is opposed to your religious convictions, you should attempt to follow the lead of the congregation. Stand when they stand, sing when they sing, pray when they pray. If there is a part in which you do not wish to participate, sit quietly until that portion of the service is over.

A Protestant need not cross himself or genuflect when entering a pew in a Catholic church. Nor must you kneel if your custom is to pray seated—just bend forward and bow your head.

If you are taking communion in a church that is strange to you, watch what the congregation does and follow their lead. When you attend another church, you should make a contribution when the offering plate is passed. This is a way of saying "thank you" to the church you are visiting.

CHAPTER 13

TRAVELS AND TIPPING

Q. *What guidelines can you give for tipping?*

A. I believe firmly that a tip should be merited. Where service is bad and the personnel rude, inattentive, or careless, the amount should be reduced. If it is bad enough, no tip should be left at all, and you should bring the situation to the attention of the manager. On the other hand, rewarding good service generously is just as important since most service people depend on tips to augment their salary. Their effort to provide excellent service should be appreciated.

For many years fifteen percent has been the accepted percentage for a tip. With this as a basic guideline, the chart below gives general standards for tipping in most parts of the United States.

When Dining

An increasing number of restaurants in the United States are adding a service charge or gratuity to the bill. You should be aware of this, and if it is the case where you are dining, you need not pay any additional tip. This practice is more common when there are six or more in your party.

BARTENDER

15–20% of the bar bill if you have drinks at the bar before going to your table. It is given to him when he gives you your check or, if the bar bill is added to your dinner check, before you leave the bar.

BUSBOYS

No tip except in cafeterias when the busboy carries your tray to the table, in which case tip 50 cents.

CATERERS AT CLUBS OR RESTAURANTS

If the service charge is added to the bill (usually 15–17%), the host is not obligated to do more unless he wishes to do so, except to the person in charge—headwaiter, maître d', or whoever it may be—who receives a separate tip of $5 to $10 or more, depending on the size and elaborateness of the party.

If no service charge is added, the host gives the person in charge 15–20% of the bill and asks that he divide it among the waiters, plus $10 or more for the person in charge.

CATERING AT HOME

Approximately 20% of the bill is given to be divided among the bartender, waiters, and waitresses by the host before they leave, if gratuities are not to be included in the bill.

CHECKROOM

Even if there is a charge for checking your coat, tip the attendant. When the charge is 75 cents per coat, tip 25 cents. If no charge, tip 50 cents per coat for more than one coat, but $1 for one coat. No extra tip for parcels unless there are many.

HEADWAITERS

At a restaurant you patronize regularly, $5 to $10 from time to time. When he has done nothing but seat you and hand you a menu, no matter how many in your party, no tip. Give $5 or more if he arranges a special table, cooks a special dish in front of you, or offers other special services.

Hand him your tip as you leave the restaurant.

MUSICIANS IN A RESTAURANT OR CAFÉ

No tip to a strolling player unless he plays specific request. Then the usual tip is $1. If several members of a large party make requests, up to $5. Give $1 to $2 to pianist or organist for playing your request.

WAITERS AND WAITRESSES

15–18% of the bill, slightly higher for extraordinarily good service. Give 20% in very elegant restaurants. If hosting dinner party of ten, twelve, or more, 18–20% percent of bill is divided among the waiters and waitresses who serve you. Never tip less than 15 cents for cup of coffee or soft drink only. Never tip less than 25 cents at a lunch counter. In a restaurant, the tip is left on tray on which check is brought or added to credit card. At a lunch counter, the tip is left on counter.

WASHROOM ATTENDANTS

Never less than 50 cents, sometimes $1 in expensive restaurant. Tip is placed in dish or plate for that purpose. If attendant does nothing but sit and look at you, no tip is necessary.

WINE STEWARD

Tip 15–20% of the wine bill when you are getting ready to leave. If wine charged to credit card separate from dinner order, a tip may be added to charge slip at the time bill is presented.

AIRPLANES

Skycaps (porters) receive $1 a bag or $3 to $5 for a baggage cart full of luggage. (No tips ever for stewardesses, stewards, hostesses, or flight officers.)

BUS TOURS; CHARTER BUSES

$5 to $10 on a long tour to both driver and guide,

depending on length of tour, unless gratuities are included in the fare. No tip for charter and sightseeing bus drivers. Optional $1 to guides or driver-guides.

CRUISE SHIPS

Cabin and dining stewards. Check with your travel agent, purser, or cruise director on the ship. Up to $5 per day or $25 per week, depending on which "class" you travel and the services you receive. Or you may tip 15–20% of the total fare, with the larger proportion going to the cabin steward and dining room steward. The remainder is divided between the head dining steward and the deck steward. Tip an appropriate proportion at end of each week so personnel has cash to spend during stops in ports.

Lounge and wine-bar stewards. 15–20% of bill at time of service.

Wine steward. 15% of total wine bill.

Bath steward. If no private bath, $1 when you reserve the time for your bath.

Cabin boy. At least 25 cents for each errand performed.

Porter. Tip $2 to $5 for heavy trunks, $1 per bag for suitcases.

Cruise director. No tip ever.

Ship's officers. No tip ever. When gratuities are included in fare, $3 to $5 to someone who has been especially helpful.

HOTELS AND FULL-SERVICE MOTELS (STAYS OF ONE WEEK OR LESS)

Bellman or bellwoman. $1 per bag—more if very heavy—plus 50 cents for opening room. Tip 50 cents per bag plus 50 cents to $1 for opening room in smaller cities.

Chambermaid. Take into account the size of your party and the amount of time you spend in the room. Adults who use the room to shower and sleep need not tip as much as a family where the parents go out to dinner each night while the children order room service. $5 to $10 a week per person in first-class hotel. $3 to $5 a week in small, inexpensive hotel. No tip if staying only one night. Give tip in person if possible. If not, leave on bureau in envelope marked "chambermaid," or give to desk clerk and ask that he or she deliver it.

Desk clerk. No tip unless special service is rendered, in which case $5 to $10 is ample.

Dining room waiter. In first-class hotel restaurant, 18–20% of the bill.

Door attendant. $1 per bag if he takes luggage into the hotel. No tip if he just puts bag on sidewalk. $1 to $3 for calling a taxi or, if you are staying longer than a day or two, $5 at end of each week.

Garage valet; parking service. $2 in large cities and $1 in smaller cities each time car is delivered.

Headwaiter. When you leave, tip in proportion to the services rendered: $3 to $5 a week if he has done little, $10 a week if he has been especially attentive. No tip needed for one-night stay.

Room waiter. 15% of bill for each meal. This is in addition to hotel fee for room service.

Valet. No tip.

Taxis. 50 cents minimum for fare up to $2.50. For higher fares, tip 15% of meter. Same for unmetered cabs; pay 15% of fare.

TRAINS

Bar or club-car waiters. 15–20% of bill, as well as

50 cents for delivering setups to your sleeping car. Dining-car waiters 15–20% of the bill and never less than 50 cents.

Luggage porters. $1 in addition to fixed rate fee. If no fixed rate fee, then $1 per bag.

Sleeping-car porter. At least $2 per person per night—more if he has given additional service other than making up berths.

GOLF CADDIES

15–20% of the regular club charge for eighteen holes, closer to 20% for nine holes.

INSTRUCTORS

No tip.

LOCKER-ROOM ATTENDANT

$1 at time service rendered if he or she provides towels or other personal attention.

MASSEUR

20% of the cost of the massage.

OTHER PERSONNEL

Generally no tip at time of service. Often a members' collection at Christmastime for employees' fund. Give additional tips, usually $5 to $10, depending on type of club and amount of service, to any employee who gives you personal attention—washroom attendant, locker-room attendants, headwaiter, etc. Sometimes additional tips may be given for special services throughout year. Guests do not tip the household staff unless residents for a time, in which case, if no service charge added to bill, tip as you would in a first-class hotel.

ANSWERING SERVICE

Minimum of $5 per operator who has a shift on your service, at the winter holiday season.

AU PAIR OR LIVE-IN HELP

One week's extra salary at Christmastime, plus small gifts from the children under care.

BABY-SITTERS

For steady baby-sitters, double an average night's salary at Christmas—or a small gift from the children is thoughtful—in addition to tip at time of service, usually the equivalent of approximately one half to one hour's pay.

BARBER FOR A CHILD

In a rural area, 50 cents. In a city, $1 or 15% of bill is about average.

BARBER FOR AN ADULT

Since the cost is higher than for a child, the tip should be correspondingly higher. $1 to $2 to the manicurist and for a shampoo, shave, etc., an equivalent amount depending on the type of shop and the number of services used. A regular customer does not tip the shop owner for each haircut, but gives him or her a gift at Christmastime.

BEAUTY SALON SERVICE

15% to one stylist who shampoos, cuts, and sets or drys. 20% if several stylists divide services, as follows: 10% to the person who cuts, 10% divided among the others. Generally no tip to a proprietor who cuts or sets your hair, although 10% is acceptable if you wish. If it is your first visit, watch what other customers do or ask the receptionist. Regular customers give a small gift at Christmastime to the proprietor, stylist, and shampooer.

BUTCHER

If you receive regular deliveries one or more times a week, tip at least $5 per service deliverer at Christmastime.

CLEANER

If your dry cleaning is picked up and delivered regularly one or more times a week, tip at least $5 per service deliverer at Christmastime.

COMMERCIAL MESSENGERS

If you use services on regular basis, $5 to $10 at Christmastime, if their service allows them to accept tips.

DAIRY

If the dairy delivers regularly, one or more times a week, tip at least $5 per service deliverer at Christmastime.

DIAPER SERVICE

$5 at Christmastime or, if you keep the service for less than one year, when you terminate the service.

FLORISTS

$1 to delivery person when you order flowers or floral arrangements sent to your home, or when flowers are sent to you by someone else.

GARBAGE COLLECTORS

$5 to $10 per crew member at Christmastime for private service. Same for municipal workers, if not in violation of local law.

GROCERY LOADERS

50 cents to $1 for normal number of bags placed in car. $1 to $2 for large week's marketing.

HOSPITAL STAFF

No money tips. It is proper to bring candy or the like that can be shared by all the staff caring for the patient. Give three of whatever the gift is, marked "1st shift," "2nd shift," "3rd shift." Otherwise the shift on duty at the time will enjoy it, but seldom leave any for the other shifts that have cared for the patient, too.

PRIVATE DUTY NURSES

For prolonged duty, holiday gift or gift on departing, but no money.

HOTELS, RESIDENTIAL

Permanent or long-term residents tip on monthly or even twice-yearly basis according to quality of service.

LIVE-IN HELP

$10 to $15 when extra work is required for large party. One week's pay at Christmastime.

PART-TIME HOUSECLEANERS

Approximately one week's pay at Christmastime.

WHEN A GUEST IN A PRIVATE HOME

After weekend visit, $5 to host's maid and/or cook for a single guest, $10 for a couple. No tip ever to servants at a dinner party.

LAUNDRY SERVICE

If regular pickup and delivery, at least $5 at Christmastime.

LETTER CARRIERS

According to the United States Postal Service, it is illegal to tip your letter carrier.

MOVERS AND FURNITURE DELIVERERS

No tip for one or two crates or pieces of furniture. For larger loads or if movers perform special services (put furniture in place, lay carpets, etc.) at least $10 per person.

NEWSPAPER CARRIERS

$5 to $15 at Christmas, depending on number of days carrier delivers and the quality of service. 50 cents per week paid at time of regular collection.

PARKING ATTENDANTS

$1 to attendant who delivers car from garage in small cities; $1 to $2 in large cities. When you rent garage space monthly, attendants are not tipped for delivery but are given tips at Christmastime and occasionally throughout year for special services, usually $5 each time.

SHOESHINES

50 cents to $1 for shoes, $1 for boots at time service rendered.

USHERS

No tip at movie theater, concert hall, opera house, or theater. $1 to $3 per party at an arena, for boxes and loges. No tip necessary in upper balconies and bleachers.

RESIDENTIAL BUILDING STAFF & EMPLOYEES *at Christmastime—depending on size of building and amount of services.*

Superintendent. $50 to $100 if he lives in, less if a janitor or other staff member does repairs.

Door person. $35 to $50 to each doorman, plus occasional tips of $1 to $5 for special services, hailing taxicabs, accepting deliveries, etc.

Janitor. Janitor or regular handyman, $10 to $20 depending on amount of service rendered.

Elevator operators. $10 to $20.

Q. *Do I calculate my tip before or after the sales tax has been added?*

A. It is permissible to calculate your tip on the amount of the bill before the tax. However, many people choose to figure the tip on the total amount of the bill, including the sales tax. Of course, as the price of meals increases, the sales tax is correspondingly higher, a fact to keep in mind when you decide on the tip.

Q. *I'm vacationing in Europe this year. Is tipping there done the same way as in the United States?*

A. No, generally it is a different system. In most European restaurants and hotels, a fifteen to eighteen percent (approximate) service charge is added to your bill. When this is done, you are not expected to give additional tips. Do not tip the bellboy, maid, or concierge. Do not tip the waiters beyond the service charge and, if you wish, any small coins returned to you as change.

When no service charge is added to your bill, or if you think the service charge is too low, tip exactly as you would in the United States.

Q. *Recently I had to buy a new refrigerator and then a new furnace. I also had new carpeting installed in my living room. I was very unsure as to whether I was supposed to tip the workmen who delivered and installed these items. Should I have done so?*

A. It's wise to touch base with business managers in these areas to see what expectations and trends are. They say that a tip is never to be expected, but when given it is received with appreciation. The best rule of thumb is that service and installation personnel who are particularly thoughtful; who take care cleaning up after themselves; who take away with them old appliances, carpeting, or materials; and who deal with children, pets, and other intrusions on their work with kindness should probably be tipped. It goes slightly against the grain to tip people for doing their jobs, but this is exactly what we do when we tip the barber or the porter who carries our bags. Delivery persons and installers are indeed doing their jobs, but these days we often thank them with a tip for doing them well. The amount to be tipped depends on the amount of work done, but generally is $5 to $10 per person for basic delivery and placement or installing.

When a job is complicated or the work intricate, such as the laying of carpeting on a stairway, the chief technician or installer can receive up to $20 and his or her assistant $5 to $10. Be sure to check the bill before tipping, however. A refrigerator installer will charge extra for hooking up a water line to an automatic ice cube maker. Since you are already paying for this service, your tip, if given, should reflect his overall work and not be based on something you may think is an extra effort on his part, but is actually being billed to you anyway.

When a delivery or installation comes at a time when you don't have cash on hand to give a tip, business owners tell me that it is not uncommon to add an extra amount to the payment of the bill for the purchase with a notation that it is to be given to the delivery or installation personnel as you designate.

Q. *How can I "tip" people who provide care or service to me and my family when it would be inappropriate to give them money? I am thinking of such people as my children's teachers or coaches.*

A. You can always remember these people with a small gift during the holidays, at the end of the school year, or after the completion of work. Remember, however, to pass on your thanks, praise, and commendation not only to the person but to his or her supervisor.

Q. *The space in coach class on airplanes has gotten tighter and more crowded. I think it is very rude for the passenger in front of me to recline his seat back abruptly and to do so without asking me first. Am I wrong in asking him to put it back up?*

A. No, you may certainly ask him, in a polite way, if he minds putting his seat up a little, as the space is too tight for you to even hold a magazine in front of you. Asking of course is all you can do. It is no guarantee that he will accede to your wishes.

Q. *It drives me crazy when people getting on airplanes hold up the passenger boarding line while situating themselves in their seats and storing carry-on bags into overhead compartments. Waiting for someone to put on a sweater or rummage through a bag while blocking the aisle gets me steamed. Is is rude for me to ask them to store their things after passengers have passed by?*

A. I do agree that there are inconsiderate and unaware travelers who don't think a thing of holding up the other passengers in the boarding line. You certainly may ask—politely and with a smile—if they would mind moving into their space to let passengers by. If you just wait a minute, however, those passengers who hold everyone else up do finally take their seats. If they don't, the flight attendants usually help to speed things up.

Q. *How can I make sure my young children are on their best behavior on a prolonged plane ride?*

A. For many children, flying in airplanes is an exhilarating experience; for others, however, it can be terrifying. You never know how your child will react to the experience of flying until his first airplane ride. But you can take some precautionary measures to ensure that the ride will be as painless as possible for all concerned. Bring along your kids' favorite toys, books, and games to keep them occupied. Pack snacks, gum, or beverages to help keep little ears from popping on takeoff and landing. Discuss with your pediatrician before the trip whether any other preparations are warranted to ensure comfortable travel; some children may need to take medications to prevent ear discomfort or nausea. Be sure to discuss the experience of flying before the big trip—let your little ones know what to expect, and portray flying as a fun, positive adventure.

INDEX